Enlightened Business

Stephen Kirk is a rare man who always looks through the superficial and sees the truth. His perception and sensitivity forces one to be honest about one's own motives in every situation. His quiet, contemplative manner emboldens when tough decisions need to be made. His robust and strong moral compass empowers one to take the difficult or path less travelled. I consider myself privileged to have worked with him and to know him.

ETIENNE DE VILLIERS, Chairman BBC Worldwide

We are taught to believe that to be successful at business you need to be aggressive, driven and highly competitive. Enlightened Business *says something different. Business can be joyful, light. Your competitor is not an enemy. Treat him or her as someone who is collaborating with you in the search for a better product or service. Being truthful and honest with yourself and others will help you to avoid tedious negotiations and heavy lawyers' fees. Make sure that deep down you really want to take that risk or make that investment, then live with your choice without regrets or recriminations. Above all, make your benchmark of success the value you create for others. That's what I got out of* Enlightened Business. *I recommend it to you.*

DAVID GRAHAM, Media Entrepreneur, Journalist and Businessman

Enlightened Business

STEPHEN KIRK

DERWEN PUBLISHING

PEMBROKE · DYFED

First published in Great Britain by Derwen Publishing 2009.

Derwen Publishing
3 Bengal Villas
Pembroke
Dyfed
Wales
SA71 4BH

A CIP catalogue for this book is available
from the British Library.

ISBN 978-1-907084-03-4

Design and production by David Porteous Editions.
www.davidporteous.com

Printed and bound in the UK.

Contents

Stephen Kirk can be contacted at stephenkirk@email.com
Also see:
www.stephenkirk.org

Introduction: Waking Up

Insanity: doing the same thing over and over again and expecting different results.

Albert Einstein

The day I met Robert Maxwell he clambered onto a sprawling oak desk in his inner sanctum at the Mirror Group and played an Alpine Horn for me. The horn was a good seven feet off the ground and it took pride of place because it had been given to him by a Swiss bank in recognition of granting him the largest loan in their history.

Now Maxwell was a bear of a man and the desk creaked under his weight as he puffed on the horn. The noise was so penetrating that a lieutenant entered discretely by a side door to ensure the 'Old Man' was still in good shape! It was a bonding moment, and I was sure I'd clinched *the* deal.

My company, Broadsystem, was the leader in providing telephone services for newspaper call-in lines and our main contract was with the Mirror Group, which was a competitor to Murdoch's News International.

When I started Broadsystem we were the only major player servicing newspapers and this was a licence to print money. However our dominant position was soon recognised and competitors sprang up, which caused our margins to be squeezed. Moreover, services became more sophisticated leading to increased software costs and investment in technology, which ate at our profits further.

My personal finances were stretched as well. My success had gone to my head and I'd bought a huge house for my family with a massive mortgage. House prices were falling and my investment was now worth less than the mortgage (sound familiar? – this was 1989). I had to do something fast in order to save my company and also pay off the mortgage. The only solution I could see was to sell Broadsystem to a media group – which is how I found myself in the hallowed halls of the Mirror Group before its eccentric owner.

Following the excitement Maxwell eased himself down and we had a short conversation in which he showed interest in buying my company and promised to be in touch. I never heard from him again – probably because he had other, bigger distractions. A few months later he was caught out perpetrating a fraud involving Mirror Group pension funds and shortly after that was found drowned under suspicious circumstances.

Anyway, none of this got me nearer to selling the company and raising cash, but as I was full of youthful enthusiasm I didn't worry too much and I believed something would turn up – and so it did.

A few weeks after my meeting with Maxwell we had a major computer outage in the middle of a huge Daily Mirror telephone competition and callers could not get through to enter. The editor went ballistic and threatened to cancel our contract. In addition our switchboard was bombarded with calls from irate clients.

In order to escape the frenzy I crawled under a desk to hide, somewhat to the consternation of my staff and secretary. I hid there for about ten minutes – this was surely the end of the line? – then my secretary appeared alongside me clutching a phone and whispering that the Managing Editor of *The Times* was on the line.

The Times was a News International title with whom we had a small contract, and so it was with some trepidation that I took the call.

'I hear you want to sell your company,' said Michael Hoy, the Managing Editor.

'Er, yes,' I replied sheepishly.

He told me to meet a News Corporation executive called John Evans at the Stafford Hotel that afternoon. Evans was an exuberant Welshman who was fond of tall stories. I spent thirty minutes joking about before getting to the point and then as soon as I started talking about Broadsystem, Evan's eyes narrowed. He focused intently before asking me a few penetrating questions and after a long interrogation, simply said:

'You should meet Rupert.'

A few days later he arranged a meeting in the News International 'fortress' at Wapping, East London, where Murdoch was friendly but surrounded by an entourage. After another short, incisive questioning where Murdoch displayed an uncanny grasp of my business, we agreed a price for my company and four days later exchanged contracts.

It was during this period that I also learnt a lot about business they don't teach you at business school. To put it in a nutshell, it's like this:

Your inner voice is a link to your destiny. If you *follow your dreams and don't compromise*, you will be lead on a fulfilling life journey. It may be scary at times, but life will never be boring and you won't become complacent!

I had always wanted to meet Rupert Murdoch and I believed that one day I would, so when it happened I knew I was fulfilling part of my destiny. Some would say that it was all down to *coincidence,* but I have found that coincidences multiply when you're in the flow, as any 'lucky' and 'successful' person will tell you. In addition *omens* guide you in the direction of your destiny or protect you from ghastly errors – if you're prepared to be open-minded.

I wish I had remembered these lessons because as the years passed, I forgot my goals; I became less honest; I indulged in politics; I became interested in status so that I could 'beat' my peers; I lost interest in my friends and family; I judged others by whether they had money or a high-powered job. I was a little git and it wasn't long before I had my come-uppance...

In 1999, I sold my stake in a joint venture company back to News International and went out to celebrate with my senior managers. We went to a local Indian restaurant and I felt ghastly. My body weight was less than seven stone, I had no appetite and for the past few months I had spent every night running back and forth to the bathroom. Not out of nerves, but because I had a serious problem – not that I knew it then.

Sitting at that restaurant table, my mobile rang. It was my bank congratulating me because the first million pound instalment for my shareholding had been put into my account. It couldn't get any better from a career front, but a little voice inside was whispering, 'You'll be lucky to be able to spend it.'

I rushed to see a family GP who diagnosed me with colon cancer. Much later, as I lay helpless in the recovery room immediately after an operation, I reflected upon what had gone wrong; that by a process of small steps I had become extremely miserable and was wasting my life doing things I didn't enjoy – and for what?

I realised that I had to make radical adjustments to how I lived my life in general, and how I did business in particular. My whole self-worth had become totally identified with my job and my bank balance. I realised that if I were to be cured I would have to change. It was then that I remembered that I had set out in business with a sense of lightness. I had resolved to be myself, to have integrity, to be egalitarian and not to indulge in corporate politics but rather to remember the higher good.

In short, I had woken up to *Enlightened Business*.

But the business world had not changed with me and in the years since I made my resolution there has been a very public growth in spiritual bank-ruptcy, an increase in cynicism and a growing disconnection between basic trading, which connects people and enhances life, and today's capitalism, which has made an art form of abstraction and greed. In this post-credit crunch world the sheer scale of global debt is unknown, and fear and panic can wipe out the livelihoods of millions of people across the globe in an instant.

All this would be understandable if it made people content and fulfilled, but the reverse is true. Executives at every level have compromised their values and become depressed, stressed and disillusioned. The long hours that so many of you work have been 'rewarded' by financial meltdown... The results are staring us in the face!

We tend to think of ourselves as disconnected from the world around us, but everything we do, say or think has an effect. A positive idea will make us feel excited, a sincere kind word will make those around us want to build our dream with us. The right actions can create Apple, Microsoft, or Triodos Bank. All these companies started with thought and intention – but all of them required market forces to be with them and the timing to be right.

We are born with genetic traits and personal preferences. We are influenced by our culture and our experiences. The world around us exhibits rhythms from the alternation of day and night to market cycles. If we can put ourselves in the flow of these cycles and natural preferences then we will find our *destiny*, the path of least resistance to our full expression.

We can then use the momentum of nature and the current financial crisis as an additional resource in creating a sustainable future. However if we work against evolution then we court a catastrophe of our own making.

While nature is trying to grab our attention there will continue to be growing intensity and volatility. Market crashes will be even more spectacular and natural catastrophes even greater until we realise that our time on earth is not guaranteed. We need to use all our creativity in order to resolve our current global dilemma. We need to attune ourselves to the natural order and then we will discover commercial and profitable opportunities that do not conflict with the universal flow.

As this book will show you, business isn't all about the money: it's about sharing your fulfilment with your customers, suppliers, shareholders and employees alike. Once you realise that business is about connecting, you will feel uplifted. An executive practising Enlightened Business at any level in a corporation will exude happiness.

All of which reminds me of Bruce Gyngell.

When I first met him he was popping on his socks as I entered his office in 'Eggcup house', HQ of the breakfast television channel TV-AM. He had just had his morning workout on the small trampoline that held pride of place next to his desk and he was perspiring gently. It was 1992.

As Bruce buttoned up his pink shirt, he launched into a monologue as though we'd been friends for lifetimes. Bruce, or the Pink Panther as he was affectionately known due his fondness for the colour, eventually cut to the chase. We discussed how my company could introduce TV phone-in competitions for his network, which would have the double benefit of being popular and generating money for the shareholders in the closing months of the company's operations.

TV-AM was about to lose its franchise because it had been outbid in an auction for the breakfast television spectrum. Bruce, true to form, had refused to submit a bid that he thought would make the company unprofitable and its successor, GMTV, would struggle for years to attain profitability.

Bruce was renowned for his eccentricity. He insisted his staff wear colourful clothes; he painted his office pink; he hired a new director of programs after consulting their horoscope, and he would oscillate between a macrobiotic diet and steak at the Dorchester Grill. The TV-AM building itself could have been built to house his huge persona. The architect, Terry Farrell, designed the atrium to depict the sun's travel from east to west, representing the early morning – the time for a breakfast channel – and the roof was adorned with 12 gigantic plastic egg cups.

Bruce could also be ruthless and in a dispute with the television union ACTT, he ran the station almost single-handed. But whatever he did, he was true to himself and people respected that, even if they did not understand or agree with him. We did a deal then and there in his office and I left the building slightly dazed. I was in awe of Bruce's magic. He was straightforward, enthusiastic, and creative – and I wondered why business couldn't always be like this.

A few years after I first met him, Bruce picked me up at Ravesis Hotel at Bondi Beach, Sydney and we walked along the magnificent coastline to Bronte. This is one of my favourite walks in the world. It was early morning; the sea was pounding the cliffs as the surfers rode the waves. Everyone we passed said 'G'day Bruce,' because he was the first presenter on Australian commercial TV back in 1956 (when he famously said: 'Hello everyone, and welcome to television') and was therefore a 'celebrity'.

As we neared the end of the walk, Bruce balanced on one leg – someone had told him this was a good exercise – and proclaimed: 'All I want is to be the best Bruce Gyngell there will ever be.'

You and I can't be Bruce Gyngell (1929 – 2000), but we can be the *best* we can be – in the business world as in the 'real' world – and that's why I've written this book.

Enlightened Business will help founders, entrepreneurs, senior executives, investors and all kinds of people who want to make a contribution to better understand the true role of business in our lives. This book is an invitation to embrace business as a powerful tool to express who you really are, and to make the world a better place as a result.

I hope you – and we all – can rise to the challenge.

Stephen Kirk, London, 2009

Chapter 1

What's Enlightened About Business?

And to love life through labour is to be intimate with life's inmost secret.

The Prophet by Kahlil Gilbran

What's the point of business?

I suspect that many of you may struggle with this question, which highlights my point. With the current meltdown in the financial markets our faith in business as usual is gone. It has been eroded in a process of small degrees over decades as we have lost sight of the *role* of business in the world.

Business is this: You have something I want and you're willing to sell it, so how much do you want for it? Or maybe I can give you something in return through 'bartering.' Bartering is entirely logical – it's the idea of money that's the grand illusion, because it's based on a global belief system. You buy into the belief that a piece of paper is 'worth' $10 and more mysteriously, so does everyone around you. You then have a currency, which can be used to buy a Starbucks chai latte, or an airflight, etc.

Normally, the belief system holds up across your community and between whole nations – but occasionally it breaks down – as it is doing right now! You wouldn't want Icelandic kronas paper unless someone paid you, preferably with the dollar.

This magic trick is taken even one step further with the drive towards virtual money. Nowadays we can move funds around electronically and we all take on trust that our bank will provide our funds for transactions, even though we can't see the paper money. In fact its quite probable that you will never set eyes on all your own money at any one time!

Extraordinary I know, but in entrusting our banks with our money we allow them total freedom to pledge our funds in whatever way they choose. And because bankers have taken wilder risks – because of pressure from you and me wanting material assets we can't afford – the system is creaking at the seams with governments scrambling to take us back to where we were, rather than asking basic questions about our value system.

So financial markets (upon which business is based) are not in themselves logical. Market prices vary according to factors more connected to what I term *consciousness* (what's in the air), than hard facts – assuming these were available.

From a holistic perspective business, like any human activity, is a way to give a means of creative expression. A secondary purpose is to earn a living – and it is always that way round.

First, there needs to be a feeling of connection – and a career should be light, fun and interesting. There should also be balance. If you spent all your time on any one pursuit at the expense of others, you would not be a rounded individual. But this is exactly where we are in the business world.

Now it might be excusable if we were all struggling to earn a crust, but many people have been earning substantially more than a living wage and still subjecting themselves and others to abusive working hours. The reason is that capitalism encourages the accumulation of money as a substitute for happiness – and in the race for money we lose ourselves.

Until very recently I was caught up in this illusion myself. I love business, I love making money and I'm good at it. I've founded three successful companies and made significant sums of money – but I wasn't happy. Only when my own life was in mortal danger due to my obsession with business did I realise there must be another way.

I discovered that the purpose of business was to give me an outlet for creative expression by means of trading. And this creative expression was more important than the money, because it enabled me to be myself, to express my essence. And this is what *'Enlightened Business'* means, in broad strokes.

Keeping it simple

One of the fascinating aspects of trading is that it's all about people and how much they like you and you like them. In the UK and the US this point seems to take a background role – even though I'm sure it was absolutely necessary for Rupert Murdoch to like me before he even considered buying my business. In parts of Europe and Asia you simply cannot trade unless you are prepared to get to know your staff, client and suppliers intimately: to celebrate and commiserate with them; to laugh and joke and to have warm and sincere feelings about them.

However as companies get bigger and the distance from customers expands, it becomes harder for any organisation to remember whom it is serving. The forces acting counter to Enlightened Business are those that encourage isolation and disconnection from the customer and whose models are remote from pure and natural trading.

For instance; once my company had been acquired by News International, it seemed harder to make money for my new owners because of the obstacles I had to circumnavigate in the organisation. I would be continually fighting internal battles against colleagues whose motivation was unclear. This is not a criticism of News, which is one of the most dynamic and successful companies you will ever come across – more a reflection on what happens in any large organisation these days.

Once my company was acquired I had to report into a hierarchical system and although I was pretty near the top of the ladder, I was prohibited from making large autonomous decisions. Worse, instead of acting on my intuition, I had to waste energy on making intellectual business cases – all good management practice, of course – but when your intuition is shouting at you and nobody else can hear, it's pretty lonely.

For example, years before Skype (the free internet phone service), I worked out that the internet would be a disruptive technology to phone companies and set about advocating that News should launch its own telephone service backed internationally by News Corporation titles (including The *Times, Sun, Sky* and *Fox*). Nobody else got it and I ended up being known as the Resident Genius or Eccentric – depending upon whether I was in the room or not!

Furthermore, when companies grow bigger they seem to attract person-alities who derive no satisfaction from the success of colleagues and who seem to enjoy playing power games for their own sake. I was constantly flying round the world attending high-powered strategy meetings and we would agree on various actions – then nothing would happen! Of course, if you work for a large company, this may all seem second nature – but to me it was astounding. I realised that the game was all about how close you were to Mr. Murdoch!

I have to confess I played this game for a while, but I was pretty crap at it and nearly got fired in the process. I also became considerably chastened and downcast as I ignored my heart and stayed at News, when really I should have been starting new independent ventures.

Enlightened Business demands simplicity and integrity, and this is encouraged by spreading as much power as possible down to the grass roots and empowering people. It means having an understanding that the organisation is one family with everyone pulling together for the common goal.

Today the opposite is happening. Executives are being overwhelmed by targets they cannot meet, budgets they cannot make and systems that do not work. They have to learn the art of deceit and obscuration and this is ultimately harmful to them and their companies. The financial 'industry' has taken abstraction to a new level, inventing 'products' that cannot be explained to the layman. You'll have noticed, for example, that the papers have recently been full of articles about hedge funds and short selling and other 'instruments' that allow ever-greater sums to be borrowed without accountability.

In the pursuit of greed, various financial 'derivatives' have been invented to allow gigantic loans to be made. Stephen Green, Chairman of HSBC said at a conference in Dubai in October 2008: 'The complexity and opacity of certain financial instruments reached a point where even senior and experienced banks had trouble understanding them, let alone investors.' These practices run counter to truth, simplicity and honesty, which are the bedrock of successful long-term business.

We can all feel instinctively that something is wrong with the system as it is, but you may feel that putting business in a spiritual framework is still somewhat of a stretch. But what then, *is* enlightenment? And is it really possible you can practise it in *your* business?

Enlightenment Now

Enlightenment can be seen as a cultivation of the nervous system so that we can actually perceive our connection with other people and the world around us as a concrete reality.

Many books are now being written about enlightenment, including Eckhart Tolle's bestselling *The Power of Now*. It is also, dare I say it, good business. In March, 2008, Oprah Winfrey and Eckhart Tolle collaborated on a series of webcasts (sponsored by Skype, Post-It Notes and Chevrolet) based on his writings. Here's a press statement from the show:

'Monday night's webcast was one of the largest single online events in the history of the internet. More than 500,000 of you simultaneously logged on to watch Oprah Winfrey and Eckhart Tolle live, resulting in 242 Gbps of information moving through the internet. Unfortunately, some of you experienced delays in viewing the webcast.'

Luckily you don't have to practise yoga or meditation to practise Enlightened Business (although it may help!). The basic principles – simplicity, unity and connection – can be appreciated by anyone.

For instance, it's really difficult to 'murder the competition' when you are fond of them! When we treat business as a battlefield, it is easy to rationalise feelings of hostility to our competitors, staff and shareholders. But business is not warfare and those who perpetuate the myth that it is are playing a large role in dehumanising trading, which is an integral and natural part of our society.

So Enlightened Business is not a withdrawal from everyday life – it is in fact, a deep connection with it. It's not difficult to find either. Go to your local Farmers Market and watch. Maybe buy some organic carrots! A straightforward trade takes place between the buyer and seller; there's banter and a sense of satisfaction for both sides. You might chat to your neighbours in the process and bump into an old friend.

There are a number of reasons why local markets are growing in popularity. People like to know where their food is from, that it hasn't travelled for thousands of miles and been tainted by chemicals along the way, or whilst it was being grown. But they also want the direct interaction that this brings and the human companionship, because business is essentially about the need to interact with others.

You won't buy something from someone you don't like – if you can avoid doing so! But you might buy something you don't need if you find the salesperson cute. I am stressing the basic aspects of trading because you can immediately see, I hope, that there is tremendous scope for warmth, compassion, comradeship and kindness at its basis.

I also ask you to consider how far your career or business life has veered away from this. I doubt that you would describe the current business environment as warm and cuddly, and I suspect that most people would not describe their company as nurturing. If you can, you are very blessed! Therefore, it should be no surprise that business, as it is currently practised, often produces strain.

The Wikipedia definition of business defines the term as: '*the social science of managing people to organise and maintain collective productivity toward accomplishing particular creative and productive goals, usually to generate profit.*'

'Usually to generate profit' is the pertinent term here. It would probably seem illogical to most of us to see the phrase 'usually to generate happiness' (as the system in Bhutan once did), or even 'usually to generate happiness and profit.' But why is this? It's because there has been a gradual shift from business being about enhancing the lives of individuals to a narrowness about making money – and only money, almost at any cost. When this happens humanity goes out the window.

Have you noticed that the happiest societies still live and practice a direct connection between everyday living and nature? In Bali, for example, every shop will make a little offering of flowers and incense and place it on the pavement outside the premises at the beginning of the trading day, and the first customer will be considered lucky and offered a discount.

In the West we tend to dismiss these rituals as superstitious, whilst disregarding the fact that they actually enhance the shopping experience. However, to the Balinese, their traditions represent an unbroken line between themselves and their culture and are carried out with lightness, charm and love.

At this point it is worthwhile to discuss the difference between Enlightened Business and cultural ethics.

The Ethical Dilemma

Ethics begins when thinking stops. Ethics evolve from belief systems that are adhered to geographically. For example, most cultures agree that murder is wrong, but even within that 'rule' there can be discussion about whether it would be valid in self-defense, or whether pre-emptive killing is valid to avert a larger tragedy.

This was an argument deployed in justifying the Iraq war, but which lead to considerable global controversy. But to bring this back to business, let me describe a couple of incidents that captured my attention and are relevant to the discussion.

A few years ago I was approached by a charity that raised significant funds to help kids in underdeveloped countries through events such as rock concerts. In the past, costs had not been covered by the income and the charity had basically relied on a few individuals to make up the deficit and to make a small donation. The events, however, had world-class acts and so one of the fundraisers, rather tired of putting his hand in his pocket every year, decided it would be a good idea to sell the rights to these events to a commercial organisation who would be able to run the actual concerts (ticket sales, merchandising) on a profitable basis, whilst money would be raised during the events for the charity.

My assistance was sought in finding the commercial organisation, but I immediately had a gut feeling that I couldn't undertake the assignment. I rationalised this as a discomfort with the crossover between the commercial and charitable ideals, and also I did not like the idea that the commercial organisation would be allowed to keep the profit, which according to the projections (which I didn't really believe – but that's another story!), would be substantial. So I declined, and felt a sense a relief.

But this does not mean that the concept was wrong. Indeed how can one have a problem when sincere people gather together and try to alleviate poverty? Nevertheless, I knew this was not for me and I was prepared to trust my judgement and walk away. Now previously, I would have difficulty in rejecting the project – the inability to say 'no' is one of my weaknesses – and I would have struggled on, wrestling with myself, feeling guilty that I was not engaged with the project mentally and carrying an uncomfortable feeling in my heart which would be acting counter to my spiritual core.

However, although this project was not right for me, there are many people who would jump at the chance of getting involved. They would be raising funds for kids' projects and meeting famous rock stars back stage – surely utopia for some? Ethics, as you will see, seems to vary from person to person.

For instance, a friend of mine was doing business in Africa and needed to have a road built to his manufacturing plant. He arranged a meeting with the government minister responsible and whilst speaking in great detail, the minister wrote intensely on a notepad. When my friend had finished explaining the project, the Minister smiled, tore off his notes and handed them over. He had written a list of people who would need to be bribed and how much would have to be paid to each recipient.

Clearly this is unethical – or is it? Maybe this is the only way to get business done and maybe the project will create employment opportunities in the region. Maybe this and maybe that – we could argue for days.

Compare this to the experience of an Italian associate. He was in the music industry, made a fortune and bought a tract of land in Puglia, Southern Italy with some dilapidated buildings, which he lovingly restored into a retreat centre. The project was completed in a year, which given the scope of the undertaking, was a near miracle. He explained that the only reason the project had been achievable in the first place was because he had been born in Puglia and his family had the right connections. This man was living his dream and as far as I could see he was a deeply spiritual person. I am sure you'll have no trouble convincing yourself this is ethical, despite the fact that if anyone from outside Puglia would have attempted it, they would have surely failed!

So ethics is a moveable feast and we humans love it because it gives us an opportunity to judge and enhance the feeling of separation that is encouraged in our culture. We can adopt an ethically superior position and feel smug. So if our company is recycling its paper we can rest easily in the safe knowledge that we are saving the environment, neatly sidestepping the fact that the same company is in the Defence Industry, say, with all the moral dilemmas this would bring.

Enlightened Business is more subtle. For a start, it's beyond judgement. Ethics and morality are about rules, whereas Enlightened Business is about *feelings*. Ethics is about *separation*, whereas Enlightened Business is about *unity*.

The Point of Connection

I am sure you've felt a time of connection. Maybe it was being with friends, listening to music, running, practicing yoga or sitting on the beach. Now imagine carrying that feeling with you throughout the day: whilst you are negotiating a contract, giving a sales presentation, or firing an employee, for example.

Enlightened Business will cultivate this feeling of belonging and connectedness amongst your colleagues, suppliers, customers and shareholders. It will fundamentally change the way you engage. For example, you may begin to desire a more collaborative approach than one of competition.

In all the businesses I started, I naturally looked for a niche that nobody else had discovered and for business partners that I could co-venture with. Needless to say, competitors soon arose and I had to fight them in the marketplace, but I always wondered what it would be like if we could work together expanding market opportunities rather than indulging in corporate warfare.

It is fashionable to believe that competition leads to a better deal for the consumer and this may be true in today's culture (although I have my doubts!), but if a company saw its customers as family then it would naturally fight to bring efficiencies and lower prices.

High ideals are often aspired to by many executives and companies, who enshrine their beliefs in their Mission Statements. The problem is that almost as soon as the Mission is written down it becomes obsolete. As soon as a set of rules is circulated they will be blindly enforced (or bent), irrespective of the context in which they were set. Evolution, or progress, is dynamic and working through us, and because it is ever changing we have to constantly review our mission and adopt new rules – and this is not an easy process.

So Enlightened Business involves constant change in an environment that fears it, and in which too often executives derive a sense of power from enhancing separation.

Now it isn't possible to examine whether a business uses enlightened principles by merely looking at a set of rules and giving a panel of experts the job of 'marking' each nominated company, thus producing a league table. Of course, strictly speaking, you could marshal a panel of experts (perhaps the Dalai Lama, Oprah, Deepak Chopra and Warren Buffet) to sit down and tell you how they feel about a list of companies, but somehow I doubt that this would make prime time television!

However, what we can judge is the degree to which a company is attempting to adopt enlightened values. In essence it's about the degree to which everyone involved in the company (including those supplying it, trading with it and its customers and the surrounding community) are able to be *themselves*.

This is not to say that enlightened companies are *always* fun! One of the difficult realisations when discussing this area is that when nature unfolds its plan, it's not always pleasurable. We like to believe that the world is essentially a 'good' place, where things happen neatly and according to our own value systems. Then when tragedy strikes, or things don't go according to plan, we see this as 'unfairness'. But life isn't like that. There are beautiful sunsets and there are also earthquakes, and 'bad' things do happen to 'good' people.

One of my most baffling business observations concerned the Transcendental Meditation (TM) organisation, to which I have been loosely affiliated since my youth because TM has brought me many benefits, especially on the creative level.

In fact two million people have paid to learn TM and many thousands buy additional programs and food supplements. So TM is at one level a business like any other and consequently its founder, the late Maharishi Mahesh Yogi, could certainly have been called a spiritual businessman, although he was far more than that.

Nevertheless, in 2003, Maharishi closed the TM organisation in the UK. This decision appears to have coincided with the Iraq war, with which he deeply objected. TM teachers were no longer allowed to teach and were consequently deprived of their livelihoods. It was still possible to learn 'unofficially' as some teachers remained active, but not 'officially'. Teaching did continue in the United States. When Tony Blair stepped down as Prime Minister, Maharishi allowed teaching to recommence.

I found this episode inexplicable. I simply could not understand how such a beneficial technique could be withdrawn. It seemed unfair and unjust, as well as causing considerable financial hardship to dedicated TM teachers. However, although I will probably never understand this decision, I have to accept that Maharishi was being true to himself in the same way as Bruce Gyngell was when he refused to bid too high for the breakfast TV licence.

When making decisions we have to follow our inner feelings, but sometimes we get confused. Let me give you some guidelines that will help you if this happens. These principles of Enlightened Business are NOT new. Although I am open to new techniques – indeed I utilise Neuro-Linguistic Programming in my coaching work – I also rely on ancient wisdom to guide me.

Ground Rules

Now let's remember some of the ground rules for Enlightened Business that we may have forgotten:

1. Think Big Picture

The world was around long before us and will be here when we're long gone – so relax!

Having an expanded vision is essential to Enlightened Business. The current culture of grasping, short-termism, and insularity is a response to the existential drama that most of us are living. We seek meaning in a meaningless world because we are looking in the wrong place. The games that we play and the accumulation of money are a distraction. We are no longer human beings but human *'havings'*.

The realisation that we are part of a much bigger eternal picture leads us to pure enjoyment and our business life can thus be transformed from a struggle into a game. And when the pressure goes we naturally become more expanded.

2. Little Me

There is a distinct difference between being comfortable in our own skin and the dysfunctional ego – so often found in business – that is working out its emotional conditioning.

Enlightened Business is synonymous with modesty. For example, business guru and multi-billionaire Warren Buffett lives in the same house he purchased decades ago, and by all accounts he is very happy there. So why does he do business? Plainly not for the money, but I imagine, for the enjoyment and the benefits he can give to society. He has, in fact, pledged the majority of his wealth to the Bill and Melinda Gates Foundation.

The current obsession we have with celebrity, the indoctrination from advertising, the need for recognition by others all feed the ego – but the more puffed-up the ego, the less easy it is to be happy. So the place to begin our reconditioning is with the ego and the process is simply to observe it in action.

After my divorce, I had to move from a large house in a 'prestigious' part of London to a modest flat. I confess, this was quite hard on my ego, but had I listened to it I would have taken out a large mortgage and watched as the price of my house plummeted in the credit squeeze. As it is, now I am living comfortably within my means and I am able to take on projects that I want. I have no debt whatsoever and my peers often comment enviously on my happiness. Many of them are far richer than I am, so I wonder why they are struggling.

Are you in a similar situation? What's your story? Listen to the narrative and ask yourself if it's true. Who is stopping you changing? Is it your ego or your essence?

3. Non-Attachment

When we start to buy into the idea that making money, or having status, or owning a particular car, or house is necessary, we are becoming attached to something outside of ourselves to make us happy. And if we can't get what we want, we suffer.

This is the one thing that most of us know intuitively but which we do not translate into reality. If we are prepared to act lightly in business, then we will discover that, paradoxically, we will have that which we wanted but no longer crave – and be more successful and happier as a result.

The curse of attachment, *the having*, runs throughout our material world. When we believe that work is mainly about accumulating material possessions then we become caught on the treadmill. Yet we see time and again that accumulation of wealth does not lead to satisfaction. There is tremendous cultural pressure for us to display our success using totems and this in turn leads to attachment to material assets and relationships.

You will understand that markets, fashion, and consumer confidence ebb and flow like life itself. By practising non-attachment to the changing nature of the world, you can focus on the value of the things which really matter.

For instance: I gave my car away about a year ago. I didn't do it, as far as I was aware, for any reasons connected with the environment, or do to with expense. I did it because it was so much *trouble*.

I no longer have to fill in forms and produce documents to Westminster Council so I can park outside my own apartment. I don't have to worry if my car will be towed away when I return from one of my long trips because they are digging up my street (again). I can walk across the main road separating me from 'Central London' without paying the 'congestion charge'. I no longer have to pay for expensive spare parts and the mandatory roadworthy certificate. I live in London, which has an excellent public transport system, an abundance of taxis and my kids are grown up, so I don't need to ferry them about. And not having a car is so relaxing!

But what is more interesting is the reaction from my friends when I told them about my car withdrawal. I began to feel like an environmental hero. And I realised how much owning a car, even in a sprawling metropolis with excellent alternatives is so much part of the 'Dream'. I specifically mention the car, because owning one is one of the central features of the Western Dream-State.

It's almost like we feel we can't be happy unless we own a car. And when we can afford a car, we get a 'prestige' model, and when that doesn't do anything for our baseline satisfaction, we get several cars. But what if we didn't care if we had a car or not? Well that's about where I am now and it's extremely peaceful. In fact, I can recommend it!

Non-attachment is the ideal state in which to function in business. It means that you are acting from your inner core. You absolutely know you are acting correctly and although you obviously would like a project or negotiation to succeed, you will face any obstacles with equanimity.

Non-attachment means acting for your own sake rather than for the perceived need to accumulate money. But as with all these values, the chance of success is maximised because acting from a position of non-attachment allows consciousness to expand so that one is aware of more factors than when one is acting from strain or grasping.

Imagine wanting *nothing*! Imagine being satisfied with what you have.

There is a misconception that this would lead to apathy – but it is equally human to want to act. The world in which we live is creative. It is part of the Creation. Very few people feel comfortable sitting on their arses and vegetating – especially if they are business people. Business people express themselves through trading. They initiate projects from the creative process in their imagination and when they are attuned they are working with evolution to advance humanity.

Why compromise yourself with attachment to the accumulation of baubles? After all, you can't take them with you!

4. Be Brave!

Fear is negative attachment and the absence of equanimity. If we fear getting fired, not making target, losing a contract, etc, then we have bought into the idea again that our welfare depends on external circumstances.

If we enter a business negotiation with a worry that we might lose the deal, this will inevitably cause a contraction and wariness which will be picked up by our potential business partner; whereas being open and relaxed will create that feeling of trust which leads to an ongoing and fulfilling business relationship.

Too much time in business is spent concerned with the downside. If we are to truly thrive we must put our attention on growth and expansion – which is where evolution is heading. People are drawn magnetically to dynamic people and repulsed by fearfulness.

Be brave, trusting and fearless in business and don't concern yourself with the outcome of your actions, safe in the knowledge that IF we are following our calling then the outcome will be taken care of and in our best interests.

5. Equanimity

Equanimity is the state to begin any business negotiation. When one enters a transaction with a clear mind, then the negotiation is in the best interests of oneself and one's company and the other party will relax into your own 'dynamic peacefulness' and will respect your openness. Negotiations from this state will maximise the chances of a successful deal.

Now imagine dealing with a failing project, an angry customer or a supplier with equanimity. Instead of a gradual upping of tension, there will be a natural flow towards harmony and resolution – even if the other side is wrong! It may be that you lose out financially this time– but this would not really affect your emotional stability, and both you and your 'adversary' will live to deal again in the spirit of give and take.

6. Trust

Now compare this with the current state of the business world. We live in a fear-based society where we engage lawyers to nanny us through every stage of a negotiation. I advocate a return to 'handshake business'. Do business with people you trust and if you don't trust them – don't do business with them!

This principle relates to everyone we meet in business. Until recently, I would always find an 'enemy', either in a competitor or in my own organisation; someone who would seem to be hell-bent on thwarting me at every turn. I really believed this was an essential part of business life and I was complaining to a friend about it – who then pointed out that in the twenty years she had known me I was ALWAYS finding an enemy. This revelation shocked me and I realised this enemy-complex was just a habit.

As soon as I began to trust more openly the 'enemies' diminished, but as soon as fear crept in they would re-appear. So a trusting nature is part and parcel of non-violent business.

7. Truthfulness and Integrity

Truthfulness and Integrity mean talking about an alignment between thought, speech and action.

I am often described as being 'direct.' I can't help myself as I am hard-wired to believe that it is a waste of energy to spend time on discussions that I know are not useful, and it is anathema to me to say one thing and do another.

However, business people I meet always comment on this aspect of my personality as though it is something highly unusual – and unfortunately it does seem to be. Every few weeks I go through my business card file and muse on the number of people who have promised to get back to me but haven't; who promised to send me a business plan or make an introduction. These are good people, but somehow there seems to be no connection between what they say and what they do, and therefore I can only wonder what they were thinking when they made their promises.

Once I was at a make-or-break meeting in Australia with a large tele-coms company and there was only one point left of disagreement: the UK was excluded from the deal. But every time the latest draft of the contract reappeared it snuck right back again. There were the usual cast of thousands at the meeting, including lawyers from either side, and by now I was fed up going over this same point. So I drew a map of the world on a flip-chart, tore off the UK, and ate it.

There was a hushed silence in the room and I thought that at last I had made my point, but on the way out I heard one executive from 'the other side' say to another: 'What do you think he meant?"

We need to be true to ourselves and true with others. If you act as truth-fully as you possibly can then it will pay dividends in both the deal and your reputation, and you will attract even more business as a result.

8. *Silence*

Here's a revolutionary thought – how about starting meetings with a period – just a minute – of silent contemplation.

In silence we are brought closer to something bigger than ourselves, and this process relaxes us and makes choice easier. Yet the business world seems to have moved in the opposite direction.

There is obviously a place for team building, away days and the plethora of activities that bring people together in the workplace and help with bonding. But I postulate that unless there is a place for silence it is difficult to open up communications that will bring a company closer together on a spiritual level.

Nor do I prescribe making silence compulsory. This clearly would be counter-productive and lead to much angry mental chatter! But the ideal way of conducting business meetings (internally or externally) would be to start with a period of silence, if only for a short time. This would have the effect of calming the environment and establishing a commonality of purpose.

I'm well aware that this will seem shocking to many people. But from my perspective it seems extraordinary that if I proposed a 10-point Action Plan it might be easier for some folk, than sitting in silence.

The common misperception is that to get ahead you have to always be available, whereas in my reality if you make time for yourself and your family and friends then you will be more balanced, clear thinking and happier.

These are the softer attributes of business that are now so easily overlooked, but essentially are what business is all about... simple trading and relationships.

9. Do Unto Others...

'Do Unto Others as You Would Have Done to You' is a wonderfully simple rule, but so rarely practised in business, even if it is respected outside of work.

How you interpret this is, of course, up to you. If you find yourself taking credit for someone else's idea, or bad-mouthing, or being overly protective of your own situation, you might like to reflect on how you feel inside. The alarm bells should particularly sound if you find yourself in an action, which you know to be wrong.

How would you respect this principle? Well, perhaps by being open and friendly to everyone, no matter what their position in the company. Or giving a colleague a break and responsibility. Praise might go a long way, too.

When I ran my own business, my door was always open and I would go out of my way to encourage my staff to come and chat. I paid for staff to have counselling, training or medical treatment. I listened sympathetically to a small delegation from our call-centre who wanted a prayer area. I challenged my staff to stretch themselves with sales targets, new products and new thinking. Several times I had to fire those who were not happy with working with us, or simply not up to the job – but in every case I tried to act compassionately and I remain friends to this day with several people I 'let go'.

The main point is that I have always tried to treat everybody I meet as family.

It didn't always work out like that, and sometimes despite my best intentions, things backfired. On one occasion, News International wanted me to replace a senior executive who had been with me for years. I should have resisted, but I went along with it on the condition that instead of firing him, I could send him to New York on an important project.

He hated me for this because he didn't want to leave his partner and go abroad. I was happy to relocate them both, but she had a job in London she didn't want to leave. Although he did go to New York, he was miserable and we ended up agreeing on a redundancy package.

I had completely misjudged the whole situation. I would have loved to go to New York – but he was in a completely different space. Had I put myself in his shoes for a second, perhaps I would have handled it better. I was also not brave enough to confront my new owners and explain why I valued this chap so highly. My lack of integrity at that time lead by degrees to great unhappiness.

The guidelines above will help us appreciate that our business skills are a gift. Once we remember that, we can allow them to play out so that they are of maximum benefit to all those around us. Once we let go of the illusion of individual doing, that simply 'being' is enough to satisfy us and that material wealth does nothing to make us happier; once we let go of these illusions – then we can play a full role in the eternal game of life.

Now here I must issue a health warning. Only you know what is right for you and the most basic rule is there are no rules. I am advocating self-referral. That is, looking inside and feeling what is right for you, rather than straining upon a particular set of values given to you by someone else.

In the next chapter we'll examine whether you're on the right path and following your destiny or whether somewhere along the lines you've gone off the rails – and what you can do about that!

WORKBOOK:

Successful business brings tremendous power and responsibility – which can be used or abused. List some examples of your own business dealings where you have used your own power – whether as an employee, manager or CEO, for better or worse:

_____

_____

_____

_____

_____

_____

_____

_____

Enlightened Business demands truthfulness and integrity at every level and can be a powerful creative tool to express who we really are. Can you remember some instances where your integrity has paid off, reinforcing your own sense of worth and winning your business a contract or bonus? Conversely, dare you be honest and list some times when your business dealings have been less than honest?

_____

_____

_____

_____

_____

_____

_____

_____

The basic rule of all life is Do Unto Others As You Would Have Done Unto You – and this applies in business as in any other aspect of life. List some ways in which you can see this rule applying in your business transactions:

_____

_____

_____

_____

_____

_____

_____

Business is all about relationships and we are most fulfilled when our business activities are in line with the flow of evolution: this is Enlightened Business. Name some of your most important business relationships – and be honest – some of the fundamental ones won't necessarily be the most obvious!

_____

_____

_____

_____

_____

_____

_____

_____

Exercise # 1

Look again at the principles of Enlightened Business. Now take a recent business day and examine how someone else might see you, particularly with regard to those nine principles:

Think Big Picture – Little Me – Non-Attachment –Be Brave Equanimity – Trust – Truthfulness and Integrity –Silence – Do Unto Others.

That other person may be your child, partner, a colleague – anyone who knows you. Really put yourself in their shoes. When you're doing this mimic how they sit – truly embody them. Imagine them talking to you from across the room – as if they were really there.

Now observe what 'they' say and make a mental or physical note. There's no need to resolve to be different (although you can if you wish). Merely thinking about yourself from another perspective will start a powerful transformation.

You could then repeat the exercise from the perspective of a different person.

Chapter 2

The Right Path?

There comes a time when you ought to start doing what you want. Take a job that you love. You will jump out of bed in the morning. I think you are out of your mind if you keep taking jobs that you don't like because it will be good for your resume. Isn't that a little like saving up sex for your old age?

From *The Tao of Warren Buffett*

When I was growing up I wanted to be a train driver, then a writer, a systems analyst and then finally an entrepreneur. So how *do* you find the path that is right for you?

In India, society was based on castes of priest, warrior, tradesman, artisan and untouchable. It was easy to know what to do in life – you just followed your father's footsteps, and most people felt comfortable doing that. This was still the expectation when I growing up in the UK.

The problem was that I didn't want to follow my father and go into the family business. My family was a long line of opticians and my grandfather had established a large spectacle frame and lens manufacturing business. The company HQ was bombed in World War II and my grandfather lost almost everything, retired and handed what was left to my father, who wanted to pass it to me.

The universe had other plans for me and I was set on a career in computers (which had just been 'invented'), but I couldn't bring myself to tell my father. And so my life headed along the direction he had mapped out for me – until a pivotal moment when we visited City University. This was the university that specialised in optics and where I was to study. My father proudly showed me the various devices my grandfather had invented, which were on display. Then one of the professors explained to me the revolution in sight rectification afforded by contact lenses. Contact lenses were the future; soon nobody would be wearing old-fashioned frames. I would have to learn how to prescribe them.

At this point, I began to feel weak at the knees: it turned out I had a phobia about eyes. To this day, if anybody starts fiddling around with contact lenses, I have to look away. I was in an impossible situation. I couldn't do the course and I couldn't confess my phobia to my father. I agonised for days before breaking the news to him, and as expected, he was devastated. He subsequently sold what was left of the business.

This experience demonstrated something to me, which is a fundamental principle that runs through our lives. We know when we are doing something that excites us and we feel passionate about; equally, we know when something doesn't suit us.

I was, however, missing one fundamental point about my family. One point that, had I recognised it at the time, would have helped me understand my dilemma. Essentially, my grandfather was a great entrepreneur. He was an inventor, a tap-dancer and a traveller, and he had a terrific sense of humour. So although I didn't inherit his tap-dancing skills, I did discover I had a longing to be an entrepreneur and innovator. So by opting out of the family business and following my heart, I was in fact being true to myself – and my genes.

A little later, in 1977, I was sitting cross-legged on a meditation course when I had a deeply non-spiritual experience that helped me find my path. An inner voice said: 'Go into business!' Now, I wouldn't say it was God talking to me, but then I wouldn't say it was 'me' either – at least not a 'me' I was acquainted with. So I did what any self-respecting spiritual seeker would do – ignore it and go back to the mantra.

However the voice was more insistent and I felt compelled to listen. I had no business training and had been making a living as a computer programmer, so I was rather clueless as to what to do next.

But as soon as I left the course a headhunter placed me in a highly paid post and shortly afterwards I was living in Amsterdam selling computer software. There followed a magical period, during which I founded a cable TV franchise, and shortly afterwards Broadsystem – my premium rate telephone business. As mentioned, I sold this to Rupert Murdoch in 1990 and worked for News International (part of News Corporation) who, in 1995, proposed a joint venture with me. Those years were like an interconnected series of dots and all I had to do was join them up to form the big picture.

But how can you tell if it's your inner voice you're listening to, or your own stubbornness or ego? I am constantly having to be vigilant when embarking on business ventures to ensure that my persistence has not been driven by my own desires. And if that's the case with you, the path will suddenly turn, or dry up, and you should be able to see that absence of flow and take heed of that message.

It's true to say that none of my own ventures would have succeeded without persistence. It took me years to finance my cable franchise and to negotiate a contract with British Telecom and to conclude a deal with Sky Television to start their discounted telephony service.

But I began a magazine even though I knew in my heart I was undercapitalised (and everybody told me so!), I took on the Chairmanship of a public company out of vanity when my gut told me to walk away, and I continued negotiations to sell my last company for a whole year instead of seeking urgent medical attention – this last bout of misplaced persistence could have cost me my life, because as I mentioned, it turned out I had colon cancer.

I am still learning. One fateful week I was offered three jobs in one day. You might think this is normal but I can assure you I considered it some sort of cosmic joke. Frankly, it's unusual for me to be offered three jobs in one year and 2005 passed me by with many meetings but none of them leading to anything fruitful.

I had no hesitation turning down the first two jobs. One was in a pre-revenue start-up and I'd resolved not to touch another start-up. The second was for an Advisory Board paid in shares rather than cash. This was a no-brainer, I'd learnt that I resented spending a day brainstorming when I could be at the movies. But the third was a public company Chairmanship and I accepted the interview.

My last public Chairmanship drove me crazy and even as I considered the position I began to feel a tightening in my chest and remembered when this was a semi-permanent feeling – not so long ago. Yet I still couldn't bring myself to cancel the interview and as the day grew closer, I began feeling more and more uncomfortable.

Then, just before the interview, fate set me up with an old friend who had been instrumental in my last resignation and I found myself relating all the reasons why this position might be suitable for me. Let me list them for you:

- It would give me an opportunity to prove (again) what I can do.
- The company was interesting and I knew immediately what would be needed to drive it forward.
- It wasn't in financial trouble (like the last one), it just needed focus and a clear strategy – and I'm good at that.
- The money – not a lot, but I could always use it.

My friend looked at me without comment and as I spouted on I felt a hollowness inside and we both laughed.

I did go to the interview, but as soon as the Founder and CEO arrived I confessed that I simply was not interested in another small Public Market Chairmanship. Small public share markets are always trouble. So what was my motivation? *Ego, vanity and status.* The three traps that haunt us in our professional and personal lives.

We are born and we die and in the eternal search for meaning we attach uncommon significance to our existence. But our existence is itself the miracle and the need for something extra is always a fruitless quest. Yet in the accumulating power and material wealth we can temporarily trick ourselves into the delusion that there is something more permanent.

My interview was short and sweet. I shared some thoughts on strategy I had been developing and walked away relieved and happy. I describe this incident because unhappiness creeps up on us. Nobody wants to be unhappy and stressed, yet so many of us become so because we are not strong enough to follow our hearts.

Let us look at this more in the business context. My feeling is that if you employ anyone or enter a deal 'against your better judgement', then it almost inevitably will end badly. It is deeply unfashionable, however, to admit this. My experience of business in America, for example, is that 'no' is almost an unknown word and becomes 'yes' by slow attrition and energy wastage. Countless meetings leading to wasted energy when a simple 'no' would suffice.

Changing Times

And then there is the subtle and under-rated quality of timing. Any decision, any strategy, any business model has its 'sell-by date'. The common tendency to set up committees and strategy groups works against intuition and action. Consequently, by the time an action is agreed, the timing might be completely wrong! Perhaps the economic environment or the market has changed, or there has been technological innovation.

Fifty years ago, change was slower, but now as we can see around us, change can happen overnight. Consequently we need to be open to CHANGE our chosen direction at all times, (including our chosen profession) in line with our inner feelings and an understanding of the market conditions. The mind will always argue for control and stability and we have to balance this intellectual activity with feedback from our heart and be prepared to change or adapt.

Geography will also play its part in dictating the correct path for an individual. For instance:

I was recently visiting India to look at a retreat project and the project manager, a young eager man with shining eyes and a winning smile, insisted on taking me back to his home to meet his mother and friends. We drove to a coconut grove on the beach within sound of the sea and under a gorgeous cloudless sky. His home was a modest three-room brick bungalow and he beckoned me to sit and offered me coconut milk whilst his mother fussed in the kitchen. I accepted, so he grabbed a machete from the hallway, disappeared outside for a few moments and returned with a large green coconut, which he lobbed off and beheaded. Mum rushed in and poured the juice and we sat back and chatted.

After ten minutes he asked, 'Tell me sir, can you help me find a job in London?'

I laughed. He wanted to exchange paradise for a nine-to-nine commuter life and I have no doubt that he will succeed. But will his life be any the happier for it?

Being Yourself and Being Passionate

The other day, I had to buy a guitar strap from a shop in Tin Pan Alley (Denmark Street) in London. Before I got there I spotted a small, cluttered shop in Charing Cross Road and wandered in to be greeted by an aging hippie behind the counter. He was beaming and obviously in love with his work. He only sold one sort of guitar strap, and that was fine by me, so the purchase was really easy. After the business act was done we chatted about life and the weather and I wandered out feeling warm and cosy. His attitude to business made all the difference in our transaction.

It reminded me of a restaurant in the 'kiss of death' spot near where I live in London. It's in a quiet road with a few shops and a pub and over the years I've watched it morph from Italian to Indian to Modern British and now French. To my amazement, the latest incarnation has survived more than three months and a friend actually recommended that my partner and I eat there.

The restaurant was packed, with a warm atmosphere and excellent food. However, what made it the most was the presence of its owner – a quirky, camp Frenchman with a gleam in his eye who was attentive, funny and self-deprecating. We'll certainly return – and he told us business to date had been 'fantastique'.

Both of these examples show the power of people who not only believe in what they do, but are also passionate.

I was never happier in my own life then when I started my own business. It was a time of great stress, but it was also a time of great excitement. My motivation was entirely clear. The bottom line was I wanted to earn enough to pay my mortgage and send my kids through school. But when I had a relatively secure, well-paid job I hated it and the first thing I did was resign. Now I suspect you will find this surprising. People have explained to me countless times how they would change their job or work pattern in a heartbeat if it were not for the school fees or mortgage.

You might find it easier to understand if my resignation was a result of deep soul-searching or weeks of agonising, but actually the decision probably took a nanosecond and was made with complete certainty and calmness and without any idea of what I would do next. And then nature conspired to send me a business opportunity, which I could enter with great PASSION and I was extremely successful.

Yet I too, was gradually seduced by the trappings of corporate life, until I succumbed to a life-threatening illness and began to steer my life back on track. So we must always be vigilant and listen to that still voice deep inside that will guide us, no matter what, if we are prepared to listen.

And if you are passionate, there will be no stopping you.

Bringing it all together

We often force our intuition into second place and we use intellect to rationalise behaviour that we feel uncomfortable with.

So what is the nature of reality? As you follow your destiny it literally becomes anything you want it to be, because what you want and what the universe wants for you become one and the same.

So let's imagine a reality in which each one of us has a special pre-ordained purpose and we know what it is.

And the benchmark for a life that honours your 'calling' is the degree to which your thoughts, deeds and actions are aligned – and if you are in any doubt, then consider whether your business life is in accord with core principles like:

- Are you truthful?
- Do you have integrity?
- Do you enter business negotiations with trust and without grasping for the outcome?

If you answer these questions truthfully, you'll be in no doubt as to the direction you should follow. Whilst business has taken on an almost religious significance in our society YOUR career should always mirror what you love, and what you do should nourish your soul.

It's true that you might have the mortgage to pay, but the 'costs' of ignoring your heart will be reflected in your circumstances. This may manifest as an issue with your health, or legal bills associated with a divorce, to name just two possible manifestations – there are so many ways nature can pull on the probability strings to bring us back to our core mission.

When examining your own career it is always worth asking who you are actually working for. Is it to satisfy yourself, or to gain respect from a parent (perhaps deceased) or to impress the neighbours? I was at the coalface for many years, and although I felt uncomfortable, I soldiered on. Then I realised that mentoring and coaching gave me more fulfillment and so I moved in to that – and now I am writing this book.

Being true to yourself is not an easy ride and it will lead you to unexpected places. But if you don't keep aligning then it's all too easy to go off track. This drift happens by small degrees and frequently involves a measure of dishonesty. For example:

- You are slightly dishonest with a supplier to improve your company's profit margin.
- You claim you are an ethical company but you know where the skeletons are buried.
- You issue an upbeat trading forecast whilst knowing you are at risk of losing a major customer.
- The work practices in some of your foreign subsidiaries would not be acceptable in Europe or the States.
- You fire someone to save costs on the orders of the Board, but make up some excuse about the employee's competence in order to feel less

guilty and lessen the risk of legal comeback.

At any stage of your business life you should be prepared to 'check in' to your internal state and to change if what you are doing no longer feels right. We have to be constantly vigilant and ensure we are not stuck in the comfort zone of a habit that served us once, but no longer suits us.

Sometimes the situation is less clear. Years ago, I worked in premium phone lines and I was very happy to do so. It was a lot of FUN! But I was constantly being challenged. Was it ripping people off, immoral, or tacky? As far as I was concerned it provided entertainment to customers, all our staff (in the early days) had a laugh, we paid well and sold out for a great price, giving our outside investors (except one) a great return. I personally reimbursed the one investor who came in late and at a premium – so that although they did not make a gain, they did not lose anything either. I was concerned to pay the investor out of my own pocket because I would rather have them feel good than harbour a grievance.

I will return to this theme later, but for now it is worth noting that the right path for one person will not be right, or even seem like a path to another. Keeping on track requires honesty and bravery.

Listening to your heart

Sometimes it's not the big issues that are the hardest to be honest about, it's the little things.

So if you have a dilemma at work allow a little time to pass until you have a handle on that niggle and can understand what it is attempting to communicate to you. We are all endowed with the most wonderful nervous system, which apart from being able to automatically organise the functioning of our body, is also able to monitor the subtle tensions that arise when we are acting against our own internal value system. This tension is like an alarm signal and we ignore it at our peril. For some people, however, tension is so 'normal' that they don't even recognise it!

Examining and resolving inner tension is the first step towards walking the right path, and it requires a fearless and truthful approach. So if you want a business life of harmony and fulfillment, but the alarm bells are ringing (or even if they aren't!), then it may be time for a little quiet introspection.

You might know the cause of your concern, but while you're at it, consider:

- Does my company share my values?
- Does it act fairly with me, with the employees, suppliers, shareholders, clients, shareholders and competitors?
- Does it represent who I am and who I want to be?
- Am I proud to work there?
- Are there any elements of business practice that I would prefer not to

think about? This is a tough one. If there are you'll have to think about them in great detail!
- If my kids, partner or friends knew how I was at work, how I behaved and what my company truly did, would they be proud of me?

If you feel comfortable after examining issues truthfully, you don't need this book and I'd certainly love to hear from you. I could learn heaps! If you're reading this because there are issues that have been troubling you and you didn't know what to do, then I'm afraid you won't be at peace until things change.

Even if you do nothing else as a result of reading this book and you sincerely want to be better at business, then BE HONEST. Being honest with yourself may be hard, but in every instance if honesty is combined with sincerity, love and compassion then you will find it will have surprisingly positive results, transform your business life and lead to a more peaceful inner life.

I invite you to read the above paragraph again slowly and let it sink in.

I emphasise again, that before acting it is imperative that you are calm. If you can address any issue with detachment, then you will be assured of a desirable outcome. Although 'desirable' here means the outcome best suited to you, not necessarily the one the ego is attached to.

The best way to effect change and to learn that change is possible is to choose one thing (*any*thing) of significance and to state your concerns clearly. You don't have to have the solution. In fact, in many ways it is better that you simply state the 'problem' openly and simply to yourself or your colleagues, Board, or investors.

I counsel *discernment* and *diplomacy* here, of course. In your time of quiet introspection when you are considering the issue, also get a feel for whom it is best to share your concerns within your company. It is important not to waste energy on idle gossip, but it is also important to honour your calling and effect change.

You can introduce the subject by a simple statement like, 'Something's been troubling me,' and you don't even have to be certain why you're troubled – but if you're simple and honest then everything will fall into place.

Once you have gained confidence and manifested one change then you will be ready for a bigger and bolder step – but the point is that your nervous system will guide you step-by-step to resolution and you will be surprised at how many of your colleagues will be relieved at hearing your thoughts.

But as discussed already, although we would like to think only 'good' happens, unfortunately the universe has its dark side and 'good' people end up doing 'bad' things.

For example, a few years ago I heard an interview with the CEO of a multinational tobacco company. It's difficult to see why anyone with a heart would work in this industry – it kills one person every eight seconds – but the guy seemed like a decent family man, a keen mind and would probably make a good friend – so I wrote to him asking how he, a seemingly sensitive man, could sleep at night with the job he did. I went on to suggest that perhaps he might consider taking his talents to another industry.

I don't know what I was thinking. No intelligent person would work in tobacco if they hadn't already justified it to themselves, but I felt compelled to write and thought just maybe I would help him switch sides – maybe help reform the NHS, or something useful.

The CEO replied that he was delighted to be working in a regulated industry. He asked me to imagine what the world would be like if it was flooded by black market tobacco. Needless to say, his response troubled me. Did he really write it – and did he believe it? If he did – deep down – then I have to respect that. I personally, would never work in the arms or tobacco industries or any company where I did not respect its core value. And YOU don't have to either. So if you can't effect change then leave, before you join the dark side.

Compare and contrast this with an example of honesty and bravery in action. I was on a bus when a school outing ascended. One of the teachers had grey lanky hair and trainers and very bright eyes. His colleague was bald and dressed in Gap. They chatted about the recent case of an addictive gambler who had unsuccessfully sued his bookmaker for 'allowing' him to lose £2m.

'Bright Eyes' recalled that his father had been a bookmaker too. When his father died, 'Bright Eyes' had inherited a small chain of betting shops and had managed one of them. Often on a Friday, a guy would blow £200 and then shortly after the shop closed his wife would appear, banging on the door. How would the kids eat? Could she have her husband's money back? 'Bright Eyes' said he felt no obligation to pay her. But something inside him was at work, because as soon as he could he sold the shops and retrained as a teacher.

So wherever we are and whatever we do, we can make choices to be what we want to be rather than being someone we're not.

We talk of our life purpose but sometimes we may feel this is beyond us. Simultaneously, though, we are in denial. We force our intuition into second place and we use intellect to rationalise behaviour that we feel uncomfortable with.

The benchmark for a life that honours your 'calling' is the degree to which your thoughts, deeds and actions are aligned – and if you are in any doubt, then consider whether your business life is in accord with your core principles.

My experience is that when conducting business, being true to yourself results in attracting business partners who have similar values; it leads to outcomes that may be challenging, but encourage growth in yourself; it allows you to sleep at night with a clear conscience and wake with passion and enthusiasm!

Bringing your values into your company

It is relatively easy to see how you can affect a company if you are the founder or CEO, but can you conduct Enlightened Business when you are working in a business unit, responsible to a macho-cultured boss or beholden to the market with demands for profit at any cost? How do you stay on your personal path when you are embedded in the flow of your company and its *karma*?

There are many who feel that the only way you can be yourself in business is by keeping things small, local and without outside shareholders. Certainly, when my business was small I had a lot of fun and I did things my way. When I sold out I eventually found myself concerned with which grade of company car an executive should be awarded, and at that point I wondered what I was doing.

But we live in a world of multinational corporations and many of you will be working for one. It's not as if everyone feels comfortable running their own business – and some of you will already be involved in an enterprise in which you have a proprietary interest. So I want the ideas in this book to be of use to anyone involved at the coalface, and I feel this is one of the most challenging issues in business today.

Andrew Simms' book *Tescopoly*, blames the British supermarket multinational Tesco for an alarming number of modern 'evils'. Whatever the 'truth', it does not mean that the people involved in these companies are anything other than good people. Whilst writing this book and reading *Tescopoly*, I went to a reception and found myself chatting to a senior Tesco's executive. I asked her what she thought about the continual criticism Tesco found itself under.

She told me she felt very uncomfortable because her colleagues were great people who really cared about their work and about doing their best. She had been working at Tesco for almost 30 years and simply did not understand the hostility. There was no doubting her sincerity and that she felt she was doing the 'right' thing. Nor am I in a position to judge. It is up to all of us to examine how we feel about how our company trades and make decisions accordingly.

But how can you ensure that others around you are on the same wavelength? How do you steer a company towards the right action when what it's probably most concerned about is its bottom line?

A good example is that of Anita Roddick, a modern pioneer of ethical business via The Body Shop, which she used as a vehicle to campaign for any issue that she considered worthy, irrespective of commercial implications.

The Body Shop's mission encompasses: social justice, straight talk, socially responsible activism, volunteerism and environmental sustainability, which inspires its stakeholders: employees, vendors, customers and the communities it touches – locally and globally. It now trades in over 500 countries and has around 2000 shops as well as The Body Shop At Home, which recruits 'consultants' to offer Body Shop products directly from their homes.

Roddick felt deeply about her principles and had to put them into practice, which is also an *enlightened* perspective. But her values were not shared by all shareholders, or even by other Board members. This led to friction within and beyond her company.

In her book, *Business as Unusual*, Anita Roddick describes how she led The Body Shop in many campaigns including: Save The Whales, Against Animal Testing and Make Your Mark (Human Rights). I was also surprised to read that although Ms. Roddick 'invented' recycling, by encouraging customers to refill their bottles, her driver for this innovation was purely financial. She wrote:

'Every element of our success was really down to the fact that I had no money... the cheapest containers I could find were the plastic bottles used by hospitals to collect urine samples, but I couldn't afford to buy enough so I thought I would get round the problem by offering to refill empty containers or fill customers' own bottles.'

What's interesting to me is that although her solution makes intellectual sense, she actually picked up on a trend (recycling) that would sweep the planet completely 'unconsciously' and at a time when the concept of customers providing the bottles would have seemed insane to any conventional supplier.

Anita Roddick also went to extraordinary lengths to ensure that all employees were involved in the business. For example, any message sent to the Board would be answered within 24 hours, and she asked employees to debate and vote on the Body Shop's opposition to the Gulf War. She also encouraged consumer boycotts of companies, whose practices she despised.

For example: when the land of the Ogoni people in Nigeria was threatened by oil exploration Roddick organised a campaign which was supported in most of the markets The Body Shop operated in. This eventually culminated in Shell re-evaluating its business practices and launching its 'Profits and Principles' advertising campaign.

Body Shop International was for many years a public company – but its ideals were not always respected by the markets. The current investment climate is profit-driven and investors have little time for bold statements unless they can be directly translated to the bottom line. In 2006 The Body

Shop was sold to L'Oreal for £652m. The Body Shop is still recognised as the UK's most ethical brand – according to their website – but I suspect their days of high level campaigning went when Anita Roddick died in 2007.

Nevertheless, by observing the history of The Body Shop, there are a number of principles that can be learnt by anyone wanting to act in an enlightened way and to stay on the right path, including:

- Enlightened Business means being brave and unorthodox
- Enlightened Business demands that you respect and involve suppliers, employees and customers in decision-making.
- Don't expect public markets to understand you – maybe Anita Roddick should have kept her company private.

Staying True

It IS possible to change your path and stay true to your core values, whether as an individual or a company. A fine example of that is General Electric (GE) – a leopard that changed its spots.

GE was founded in 1886 and epitomised the 'old school' approach of the first U.S. companies who treated their employees more like family members. Even now it combines a hard-nosed business edge with a degree of compassion, relatively unheard of today. Before the current short-term mania, loyalty to company was paramount and in return the company took care of its employees as best it could.

Jack Welch joined GE in 1960 at the age of 25 and became its youngest Chairman and CEO in 1981, bringing youth, dynamism and an unconventional approach to the role. He slimmed down the various management levels so that executives felt empowered and he imbued the company with his own passion. Welch lived and breathed GE and I am sure he saw working there as his destiny. Yet, it was far from plain sailing and in late 1970's he and GE were drawn into an environmental crisis that is only now being resolved.

Polychlorinated biphenyls (PCB's) were chemicals used as a fireproof insulating fluid for electrical products until the late 1970's. From 1947 to 1977, GE legally dumped as many as 1.3 million pounds of PCB's into the Hudson River during this period, polluting a 197-mile stretch of river.

There is evidence to suggest that PCB's cause cancer in animals and then by extrapolation in humans too – although this has yet to be proved. However, in 1976 doctors at Mt. Sinai Hospital announced the results of their study, which showed that nearly half of all workers at the GE plants had developed some type of skin problem; many of which were known types associated with PCB exposure.

And in 1977, Dr. Robert Korns published his population study on people from Poughkeepsie, NY who were drinking water from the Hudson with a high concentration of PCB's. This study showed a significant increase in the incidence of male colorectal cancer. These and other studies are important because PCB's are absorbed by humans mainly through the eating of contaminated fish and once consumed the chemical remains in fatty tissue.

Other studies have shown reproductive problems associated with PCB's and women of childbearing age and children are advised not to eat any fish from the Lower Hudson. In short, you'd be well advised to stay well clear of PCB's and there seems a clear case to clean up the Hudson.

Under the 'Superfund' Law polluters are responsible for clearing up their own pollution. But GE's internal studies found no causal link between PCB's and cancer. In hindsight it is easy to put all the blame on GE. Certainly they were the polluters. But PCB's were commonly used in industrial processes to make the consumer goods that we demand and at the time of their widespread adoption nobody had a clue about their harmful side affects.

Jack Welch in his autobiography, *JACK: Straight From The Gut,* wrote:

'GE isn't made up of bricks and mortar. It's nothing more than the flesh and blood of the people who make it come alive. It's made up of people who live in the same communities, whose children go to the same schools as the critics. They have the same hopes and dreams, the same hurts and pains.

When they're big, they're an easy target. And when they're winners, they're an even bigger target.'

If I were writing a book about corporate social responsibility or environmental policies, I could have a field day analysing the history of this drama – but luckily I'm writing here about Enlightened Business and how one can look at business from a holistic perspective.

We see that Jack Welch was fulfilling his destiny by working for GE and was on his own right path, but the larger momentum of GE totally absorbed his own trajectory. He recognized the human-ness in his employees and appeared genuinely concerned for their welfare, but you can also see his anger and frustration by the use of the word 'target' and one can't help wondering whether nature was sending him a message that would have taken some of the stress out of this whole episode, had he listened and acted differently.

Of course, the company was acting in good faith and legally when it started using PCB's. I suspect it would have claimed that PCB's lowered the risk of fire and they were therefore being highly responsible – which in context would have been true. As people, we always want to blame, judge and understand but the reality is that we do not have access to the inner minds and souls of those involved.

Certainly it is a sign of how consciousness has grown that many of us now see that dumping waste into a river (carcinogenic or otherwise) is almost seen as an act of violence, especially as the waste is later ingested by animals and humans alike.

IF there were a delay caused by anyone involved on either side (GE or the authorities) that meant there was an increase in human suffering as a result or IF there had been a lack of truthfulness and delay in stopping the dumping, or IF money had in any way played a part in blocking a quick resolution of the problem; if any of these had happened they would have produced inner and out conflicts in terms of the many consequences of this drama.

The days of the thunderbolt from heaven are few, but nevertheless *karma* (the law of cause and effect) would have played out (both positively and negatively) in the lives of all the protagonists.

So what COULD have been a more enlightened approach, given that there are never absolutes in the real world?

Clearly, dumping should never have taken place in the first place and although GE was unaware of the specific problems with PCB's, it nevertheless is responsible for the consequences of dumping in general and the health hazards associated with PCB's as long as these continue into the future. Therefore the safest course of action for GE, its employees and shareholders is for it to spearhead the cleanup as fast and as safely as possible.

Interestingly, the current Chairman of GE, Jeffrey Immelt, was described by *Fortune* magazine as the 'Tree-hugging, pinko boss of a $173 billion industrial giant,' because he is leading the charge on environmental issues. Just the man for the job, I'd wager!

For many cynics, the radical 'conversion' of companies like GE to environmental campaigners might be thought of as a ploy, but I see this kind of transformation as an inevitable consequence of the rise in consciousness and the connectedness that follows. Companies, too, are choosing the 'right path' because there is no other option in today's increasingly transparent global market.

Change on an individual or corporate level has to come from inside. Whilst there is alienation and denial between a company's actions and soul then it is left to external pressure via whistleblowers, pressure groups and legislators to force companies to take responsibility and ensure Enlightened Business practices. But this approach is schizophrenic because ultimately individuals are the building blocks that make up the company as a whole.

Still, not every company is willing or able to change like GE and even though you may have a certain autonomy in your department it is equally important to examine any niggling doubt about the way your company operates – and this applies whether you are a Founder, Board member, employee or shareholder – it is important to speak about it. Talk to your partner, your kids, friends and colleagues and let them help you get a sense of perspective.

Just listen to your heart and remember that the best time to consider life-changing decisions is when you are calm and detached. Only then can the universe 'speak to you' and you can actually start to hear it.

WORKBOOK:

Does your chosen career honour who you are you and how you want to be? Write out your dream job description – and this works just as well for the job you are in now as any other, so you can start anchoring the changes you want to manifest.

_____

_____

_____

_____

_____

_____

_____

_____

Does the company you work for have your values? Can you list your values below and then compare them to the Mission Statement or ideals your company subscribes to.

_____

_____

_____

_____

_____

_____

_____

_____

To have a successful business life it is essential to be passionate about what you do, and free from conflicts in yourself or about how your business operates. List some of the internal or external conflicts you face in your day-to-day business life.

_____

_____

_____

_____

_____

_____

_____

_____

THE RIGHT PATH?

In business you must be honest with yourself and able to say 'no'. Write down some examples of times you have not said no and regretted it.

_____

_____

_____

_____

_____

_____

_____

_____

Nature has a purpose for all of us, and if we listen to our inner voice we can align with our higher path. Reclaiming your inner voice or giving expression to it isn't as hard as it might seem. To start, list below some examples of your own intuition in your business dealings – whether you listened to it at the time or not.

_____

_____

_____

_____

_____

_____

_____

_____

Exercise #2

Find a spare day and arrange to go for a long walk with a good supportive friend (not anyone who's heard your story before – like your partner!). Go somewhere you really like and make sure you have time for a leisurely lunch as well. Identify what you love about your career and company and those aspects you'd like to change.

Then take ownership of the problem areas and discuss solutions rather than externalizing them as beyond your control. Ask your friend to challenge you. Not in an argumentative fashion, but in a constructively critical way. And be prepared to return home with an action plan.

Sometimes we scare ourselves by trying to solve everything at once. Choosing only one thing is enough to begin – providing you action it! Then emboldened you can begin to move on to greater heights and challenges.

Chapter 3

Finding Your Business Destiny

Good judgement comes from experience, but experience comes from bad judgement. (Anonymous)

From *Relax and Renew* by Judith Lasater

I was once in New York and a friendly contact arranged for me to meet a businessman who was interested in proposing a joint venture to me. The businessman – I'll call him Duncan – worked out of a snazzy office on Third Avenue and in turn reported to the founder and owner of the company. There were various niche publications on display; design, cars, gadgets, etc.

Duncan explained that his boss desperately wanted to enter the UK, but needed a business partner who knew the market well. They had a telecoms venture that they would share with me if I were willing to go in with them 50/50. Around Duncan's corner office were pictures of his family – several on his desk, and one on the wall.

After 20 minutes a slightly rotund man entered and briefly introduced himself as the owner. He was immaculately dressed in a sharp grey suit. I guess he was in his late 50s, with tanned skin and an olive complexion. He shook my hand warmly, asked about my family, made encouraging noises – and left.

I liked Duncan enormously. He had a good sense of humour – always a plus point for me and he seemed honest and open. I was also flattered that they had 'found' me, and without hesitation I accepted their proposition. I flew back to London and quickly formulated a written agreement between us. We would each put up an equal amount of money and they would lease me some proprietary equipment that they had specially designed and was in use in the States.

Shortly after the equipment arrived, I was chatting to a friend about the project and his face dropped.

'But don't you know who those guys are?' he asked in disbelief. 'They're a front for the Mafia… they need schmucks like you to launder their money!'

Aghast, I hired an investigator to do a report for me (in those days there was no internet)… And sure enough, the US authorities had been trying to pin the boss guy for years. Duncan seemed clean but had been working with the organisation since he left school many years previously.

That day, I rang Duncan in New York. I told him I'd had second thoughts as there had been negative press comments, which were worrying my shareholders. This was true, luckily!

Without a beat, he asked; 'Where will you be tomorrow morning?'

'In my office,' I replied.

'I'll be there at 9am…' and before I could respond he'd hung up.

The next morning Duncan arrived. He'd caught the first overnight plane out of New York and despite that looked calm, relaxed and glowing as he sat with me in my office overlooking Camden Lock. After attempting to convince me to change my mind, he explained politely and patiently that were I ever…*ever*… to enter that particular business sector on my own and without them, there would be *serious* consequences. I emphasised that I certainly wouldn't be bothering, but just for good measure he assured me that they would be watching *closely*.

It was all done with tremendous grace, but I was left in no doubt as to the way they viewed my behaviour. As he left for the airport, I breathed a sigh of relief… and I never heard from Duncan again. I was quite sure that Duncan was a nice guy and so was his boss – but then clearly from the report of the investigator, the organisation was behind many sleazy businesses.

I took the decision to withdraw from any dealings with Duncan because I felt that although I could make money, I would be involving myself in the activities of their company – their *business karma*, if you will – and this would have a negative effect at some level of my life. It was done purely at the emotional level – although of course there were many intellectual arguments I could have made for withdrawing – or proceeding!

This episode left me with a fascination as to why 'good' people do 'bad' things, and a resolve to better understand what 'destiny' means in relation to our business lives.

When Good People Do Bad Things

How can an upstanding member of his community like Bernard Madoff set up a massive fraud? How can the former CEO of Royal Bank of Scotland feel comfortable taking a lifetime pension of $1m (he's 50 at the time of writing) when his bank has just lost billions of pounds and investors have lost their life savings?

I also am captivated by the story of the founder of Whole Foods, which is the only supermarket I am comfortable shopping in. When I am in New York, my partner and I make a point of visiting the Columbus Circus branch, just for fun! Here's a Whole Foods history lesson from their website:

'Whole Foods Market was founded in Austin, Texas, when four local businesspeople decided the natural foods industry was ready for a super-market format. Our founders were John Mackey and Renee Lawson Hardy,

owners of Safer Way Natural Foods, and Craig Weller and Mark Skiles,
owners of Clarksville Natural Grocery. The original Whole Foods Market
opened in 1980 with a staff of only 19 people. It was an immediate success.
At the time, there were less than half a dozen natural food supermarkets in
the United States.'

Imagine that – less than six natural food supermarkets! So these guys
were onto something when they saw the future... and it was natural and
organic. Or perhaps they saw the past, because the chemical industry has
only existed since the 1950's. Before that food was ONLY pure and organic.

What do I like about Whole Foods? Well the staff care, there's a lot of
food sampling, it's laid out in an interesting way and so I see shopping
there as a form of entertainment. I believe life was meant to be fun, so this
appeals to me. Again, it's a public company, but investors understand they
are investing into a company with a clear mission.

But despite all this, the co-founder John Mackey remains an enigma and
is as example of how being 'good' does not necessarily translate into being
ethical. In fact, Mackey was deeply unethical in 2007 when he used
'anonymous' postings on electronic message boards to denigrate Wild Oats
Markets – a company he wished to acquire.

His bid was blocked and he then had to face the humiliation of an
enquiry into the postings, which culminated into an apology and a plea for
forgiveness.

Whatever we do, whether we are conscious or unconscious, whether our
action is deliberate or accidental, we must take the consequences. But
strangely, these consequences are unpredictable in the sense that they are
subject to too many variables to allow for accurate prediction.

Most of us would like to believe that if we do 'good' we will be repaid
in kind and every time we see evidence to support our belief system, we
feel better. There is some 'fairness' in the universe. We can rest at night.
But if we were to be ruthlessly honest with ourselves, we would see that
life is far from fair, and in my experience bastards in business, as in every
other walk of life, sometimes flourish and sometimes suffer – but no more
or less than those 'good' folk we see.

Because we are conditioned to behave differently at home than at work,
we can be remarkably inconsistent. A business acquaintance was a saint in
safeguarding the rights of domestic staff working in the block of flats
where he lived, but dastardly when it came to dealing with small shareholders in his company.

I've also noticed that those who act without consistency tend to carry
around a fair degree of tension and unhappiness. Therefore it is better to
identify inconsistencies and deal with them.

'Business is Business' legitimises a number of behaviours that would not be tolerated in general society. We allow ourselves to 'wage a campaign' and 'kill the competition', for example, helpfully forgetting that the 'competition' is full of people just like us – maybe some of them are even friends or relatives.

And this is the moral for all actions out there. It is impossible for anyone to judge whether an action is 'right' or 'wrong', but each of us can live our own truth, and not be swayed by other people's agendas, specifically being drawn into other folk's dramas.

Take the case of Henry Ford and the motorcar. Did he free the world or cause climate change? Is Ford ultimately responsible for motor accidents? This seems absurd on one level, but is that idea so far removed from the GE example earlier, where they are still clearing environmental damage caused by the company's actions decades ago? What is our business destiny and where does free will fit into it?

We can only assess these issues on the intuitive level.

Evolution at work

The evolutionary force works through business and each enterprise (like an individual), will have its own fate. It will be able to exercise its free will via the Board and meet resistance from market conditions and competitors. The consciousness of the company will also be changing with time and therefore we must be ever vigilant to ensure that we are not just going along for the ride, because we may not like the destination.

We would like to believe that we are in complete control of our destiny, but actually there is something bigger at work organising the evolution of our world. Nature has no trouble recognising this, but we have deep trouble. Animals rely on instinct, or what we might call intuition. We rely on intellect at the expense of intuition and at the ultimate cost to our environment.

What is required is to balance our intuition with our intellect; not to use one at the expense of the other. Nature has a purpose for every one of us, both as an individual and an organisation, and this is our business 'destiny'.

There is no free will and there is absolute free will. It all depends on your perspective. We certainly have the subjective experience of free will and we have to accept the consequences of every action, but let us look more closely at how we behave in the world.

One of the fundamental mistakes we make in business is elevating the conscious mind to a position of dominance, such that everything we do is subject to rigorous intellectual analysis and is not balanced by emotional intelligence.

The conscious mind processes about forty bits of data per second and the unconscious mind forty million bits per second. Need I say more? The unconscious mind is one million times more powerful than the conscious, but the conscious mind has 'free will'. Since the conscious mind has so little processing power, the unconscious mind has to present it with carefully edited highlights, otherwise the conscious mind would overload. And from this carefully edited information, we exercise our free will.

The unconscious will also compare and contrast every experience with what it has 'learnt' already. An event will be presented with a judgement or emotion attached based on its conditioning. As humans we also seem programmed to find the inexplicable uncomfortable. Consequently we want a reason for everything, explanations and categorisations. Therefore our unconscious is constantly making assumptions in a sort of 'If it's Tuesday it must be Paris' sort of way.

So we are preconditioned from the moment we enter the world as a foetus. Elena Jazin from the University of Uppsala (the oldest university in Scandinavia) has determined that mental traits differ between men and women, including: empathy, aggression, risk-taking and navigation(!). Taking this at face value you can see how we are pre-programmed to react in certain ways simply by virtue of our sex.

Then as we progress as babies we listen and learn from our parents and are programmed to respond in certain ways. Our mother tells us to look both ways before we cross the road and to beware of strangers. Our teachers tell us to write neatly and put our hands up before we go to the bathroom. When we are brainwashed sufficiently well our reactions become automatic, so that I will 'naturally' look the 'wrong' way when crossing a street in New York, and veer to the left of the road when driving there (in the UK we drive on the left – the 'right' side for driving!)

Recently I went out to lunch with a mild toothache and down the road I noticed an office with the sign 'Garth Tooth Architects'. I must have passed it a hundred times but this was the first time that my unconscious had noticed the 'Tooth' and brought it to my conscious attention.

In the same way we carry out our lives believing that we are making rational judgements; that we are sophisticated and above making knee-jerk reactions. And we are always quick to blame someone or something else when things don't work out, without accepting that our reaction to a perfectly innocent occurrence was merely a conditioned unconscious response.

Now as a thought experiment, imagine there is a computer that can hold every fact in the universe. Something akin to the computer 'Deep Thought', in Douglas Adams' *Hitchhiker's Guide to the Galaxy* books. 'Deep Thought', for those of you who are not science fiction fans, could provide the answer to 'Life, the Universe, and Everything' (which was of course, 42).

This computer would 'know' about every cell in your body, everything that has ever happened to you, what anyone has said, what you did, what you thought, how you felt. And it would have this information for everybody and everything. Then it would be able to predict exactly how you would react in any given situation. And through the eyes of this computer, there would seem to be no free will.

The surprising fact is that the computer I postulate exists. The computer is our universe and its 'software' guides evolution. The tool we have to contact the computer is our nervous system (not our mind). To decipher clearly we have to see the world without any conditioning and the conscious mind needs a direct connection to this 'cosmic computer'.

So now, what of free will? Given that we are experiencing the world in a highly selective way, you will see that the only hope you have of being truly free is either when you can see through the conditioning, or neutralise it.

So the most likely explanation of the actions of previously 'good' people like Madoff is that they allowed their intellect to rationalise their actions and their fear to propel them against the better judgement of their subconscious.

Learning The Game

When I first entered the playground of work, I had to learn the ground rules fast. It was in 1975 and I had a traineeship as a Computer Programmer in the then nationalised UK electricity supply industry. I learnt that the smarter you looked, the more seriously you'd be taken. I learnt to play 'Spot the Boss', which meant that when he appeared you had to look busy and rehearse a cogent answer to, 'so what are you working on?'

I would answer something like, 'writing a program to predict the number of birds that will fly into electricity pylons.' Which would be true. I would then point at the acres of pages of hand written computer code that some poor soul would have to type onto punched cards to be fed one-by-one into the computer. The boss would stare at my code as though he could follow it, sway up and down and then wander off rather nervously.

It was only when I was running my own business and was bored that I realised he was playing, 'Be The Boss,' which involves wandering round the office and asking simple questions like, 'so what are you working on?'

Once I was in business properly I learnt some new games like 'Poker Face', and 'Ask for More and Settle for Less' and most importantly, 'Business is Business'.

'Business is Business' allows you to be mean, screw other people, and to be dishonest to the extent necessary to win the deal or save face. For me, it's a particularly nasty game although for many years I played it. As with 'Don't Talk to Strangers', 'Business is Business' becomes such second nature that you don't even realise you're playing it.

As I've said, if you really want to have free will in any aspect of your life, including business, you have to learn to by-pass your conditioning. This isn't so easy, but you can take the first step by being aware that you are conditioned.

If you simply observe what happens when you meet someone for the first time (do you take an instant liking or dislike? Why is that?), or observe yourself becoming irritable at the idiot in a meeting, or note how you find yourself feeling pleased when someone at work you dislike (or like!) has a mishap – then you will begin to see how you are one big conditioned response.

Destiny

Most of us will have had the experience that an event is pre-destined. It may be something quite small on the surface that appears to alter our journey through life. It may lead us to a life partner, a new house or job, overseas travel or a major deal. And most of us have felt a buzz of excitement when something is 'meant to be'.

As each one of us is a player in the evolutionary process, and evolution is about growth, then we will all be set challenges. However, nature is also clever enough to provide us with the tools to face each new adventure.

It may be that we have a professional skill or that we are blessed with a special mentor. Maybe we sit in an airline seat and the guy next to us becomes a major client or ends up selling us their company.

When I founded my premium rate telephony company, I had a clear vision that I would sell it to either Mirror Group Newspapers (then a major UK media company) or News Corporation. I didn't know how, but there was a certainty. I also stress that this was not a 'visualisation'. The image appeared to me automatically in my imagination and quite surprised me, as at that time I had absolutely no contacts in either company.

As discussed above, we all have the subjective experience of free will, and when faced with a choice we are certainly free to explore the various alternatives and to go with one of them.

Some lessons are more important for us than others. Nature will work quite hard to teach us these, but we are always free to ignore the signs and opportunities.

For example: I believe that it was my inability to follow my heart over the years that made it necessary for me to experience cancer. This helped me to be brave enough to undergo the transformation required to put my life back in touch with its destiny. The more we are able to see through our conditioning and to listen to our inner voice, the clearer will be our destiny and the more ease and enjoyment we will have following it.

Take for example the actor Paul Newman, who combined acting with making salad dressings! Rumour has it that he was more proud of his charitable venture, Newman's Own, than his formidable acting career. We'll never know for sure as he died in September 2008 at the age of 83. Nor will we know if he would have gone into the retail trade if his acting career had faltered. I suspect so as he seems to have been predisposed to it – but I doubt that he would have been able to operate it as a not-for-profit venture had he not had a considerable financial freedom by virtue of his films.

Whatever – the fact is that Newman's Own came out of an entrepreneurial flash coupled with a genuine desire to make a difference.

Inspiration for Newman's Own came when he asked his friend 'Hotch' Hotchner to help him mix his home-made salad dressing and decant it into bottles to give the neighbours as Christmas presents.

There was some dressing left over, so the pair found a local bottler and started selling it in local supermarkets. Newman only allowed his celebrity to be exploited if all profits from the venture were donated to charity.

The slogan for the company is 'Shameless Exploitation in Pursuit of the Common Good', and the company has since donated more than $250 million to over 1000 groups.

The remarkably honest and endearing website (www.newmansown.com) says: 'How to account for this massive success? Pure luck? Transcendental meditation? Machiavellian manipulation? Aerodynamics? High colonics? We haven't the slightest idea.' The big question now, of course, is the manner in which the company will be run with its founder gone – but I am sure it will continue to flourish as the trajectory of intent Newman set up for it will blossom into its business destiny.

The Bigger Picture

Even if we are aware of our own conditioning we are still subject to cycles around us, particularly market cycles.

When I was a boy in the UK in the 1960s, workers were continually striking; the unions were all-powerful; it was unusual to be an entrepreneur; there was no venture capital industry; a job was for life; the Russians were perceived as the biggest threat to peace; there had recently been a war instigated by Germany and London was often unsafe because of IRA bombs.

Today, the unions have little power; money has dried up and the market is fragile; there is peace in Europe and a unified European currency; a job lasts a few years, and London streets are safe but there is fear of another terrorist attack; and oil prices are rocketing and falling as the wind blows.

Whenever events happen it is natural and human to seek an explanation to try and bring predictability into the randomness. But although nature has a plan, we attempt at our peril to predict it using our intellect. Nobody predicted 9/11, or the financial meltdown of 2008.

In fact, I recently asked an astrologer where I should invest my money and he told me to buy gold. So I invested in a share that tracked the gold price. The price rocketed and reached over $1000 per ounce. All the pundits (and my astrologer!) suggested that gold would rise. Some said it would reach $1500 an ounce. So I bought more gold shares and guess what? Yes, it plummeted. Luckily I got out and still made a slight profit... and now the price is soaring again!

As another example, I typed 'Soros makes millions' into Google. I got 1.7 million hits. I then typed 'Soros loses millions' and got 911,000 hits. George Soros is, of course, one of the most respected philanthropists and speculators, but even he gets it 'right' only some of the time!

So although each of us has our fate or destiny, it is unpredictable to the human mind. Our *path*, however, is predictable and we have *free will* to follow it. But don't expect that path to be a straight line. It will wind and may even go back on itself. We have *free will* to follow the path or deviate from it, but we must always take the consequences, whatever we do.

The current global financial crisis and the rising cost of fuel and food will affect our attitude as to how we spend and save, as well as the future of the banking industry. It will force us to re-evaluate our work-life balance, how much we travel and where we spend our holidays. It will change the economic model of how we shop and make local markets more attractive, thus strengthening communities. That's the bright side.

Conversely, some companies that are marketing genetically modified foods are increasing their lobbying in Europe (where such products are treated with suspicion), as a 'solution' to rising food prices. And the nuclear energy lobby (which was previously shunned) is now being touted as a cure for fluctuating oil prices and dependence on a few oil-rich states.

One thing is sure: every company and all those associated with it will have to bear the consequences of its actions. They have the free will to create their own 'karma'. In times of crisis decisions are made quickly, procedures bypassed and shortcuts taken.

But at times like these it is even more important that we tune in to our destiny.

WORKBOOK:

Do we really have free will, or are we just conditioned to respond in habitual ways? Is this really free will? List some of the ways you respond to stimuli in your business world.

_____
_____
_____
_____
_____
_____
_____
_____

Recognising our own conditioning can be hard. But if we can act from a place beyond conditioning, then we will be truly free and able to be extremely successful in business and life in general. Look at your examples above, and now write out alternative ways you could respond that aren't so habitual.

_____
_____
_____
_____
_____
_____
_____
_____

Destiny is the destination the universe has in mind for us and it gives us the lessons we need to learn. We are free to follow our calling or give precedence to our ego and go off message. List some times that, against your better judgement, you chose a path that took you off your course.

_____
_____
_____
_____
_____
_____
_____

Whatever we do, we must take the consequences – and this applies to the business world more than we realise. Looking at your list above, now try to list the lessons you learnt from going against your destiny.

_____

_____

_____

_____

_____

_____

_____

_____

_____

Exercise #3

Think about your passion for your current work and mark yourself between one and ten, with ten being orgasmic passion and one being complete loathing of your current situation.

How was it for you?

If you scored seven or more you're certainly in touch with your destiny, but if you scored less than that, use the timeline exercise I set out in the next chapter. First look at how you got to this point in time, particularly the decision points that got you here and then imagine a different scenario, where the end of your timeline is the perfect career.

When walking the timeline, there is no necessity to consciously think about each step. Simply step off the timeline and look back and see what ideas your subsconscious brings up to help you progress to a more fulfilling life.

Chapter 4

Attunement – Practical Tools

There is a silence at the heart of things. You may find it when you do not seek, but stand and wait, and like a hill or tree, are for a little while content to be. Then you may even hear the silence speak.

Christian mystic wisdom

In order to make the best business decisions we must be clear, intuitive and rational. To me, rational means the ability to perceive a situation using the best and most comprehensive information without filtering or emotional baggage. The best decisions are made from a quiet mind that is tune with its destiny.

We have discussed how our 'free will' is actually influenced by our internal conditioning. But our culture also cultivates distraction. Advertising and peer pressure contribute to our inability to listen to our heart to such a degree that many of us are unhappy and dissatisfied, without any clear indication of why. Attention span is another casualty of the information overload we are receiving from the outside world. And we take all this into our businesses and then expect them to perform well!

To be able to fulfil our purpose, we have to be clear about our objectives at every level. How many times have you heard someone (or yourself) say: 'Part of me wants to do this, but another part of me wants to do the opposite?' As we discussed earlier, the unconscious mind is the most powerful part of who we are and it attempts as best it can to please us. But when it gets mixed messages from the conscious mind, it doesn't know how to respond and it defaults to old habits.

So if we are to be powerful in business every part of us must be working together in harmony, and this is the purpose of *attunement*. We must be able to see through the conditioning and hear our inner voice above the din of mental chatter.

We have seen that although the universe proceeds perfectly through evolution, man is unique in being able to consciously impose his will over intuition. The results of this can be seen all around us. The world is in a far from perfect state due to the influence of the human race, and a certain amount of humility would be appropriate. Instead we see governments and corporations acting in ways that are having far-reaching, long-term and possibly irreversible effects.

This is important in the business world because the attitude that 'Business is Business' has indoctrinated many of us into believing that we are out of the evolutionary loop, simply because we are 'on message' for our company.

Furthermore, although social, ethical and environmental concerns may be part of a corporation's Mission Statement, it is remarkable how often this gets 'forgotten' whenever profits are slipping. This is particularly the case now, in the midst of a credit crunch and with food prices rocketing. As long as a company's success is solely about profit, then it will be impossible to keep holistic issues in perspective.

I'm assuming you're reading this book because you want to make a difference and not compromise your values. This doesn't have to be as hard as it might sound. In fact, what follows are some ideas and tools that I hope you will be able to incorporate into your business life.

The Narrative Fantasy

One of the side effects of being human is the endless stream of thoughts the conscious mind produces. Because it is human to want to control and explain things, a lot of our mental activity is involved in story telling, linking cause to effect. This 'narrative fantasy' world is something all of us inhabit every day of our lives. These thoughts relate to the past and future and are filled with our hopes, fears and idle gossip. They aren't about the now, because the now just *is*.

There is a curious transformation that occurs when one is truly present – and it's a state that we can work towards. Being permanently in the *Now* is what in spiritual traditions is termed 'enlightenment', or 'liberation'.

Although we may or may not reach this state in our lifetime, it's something that we can aspire to. Various practices, such as meditation, help us to quiet the mind so that we can tune in more clearly to the voice of the Universe. The 'conscious' mind is simply a repository of filtered information as presented to it by the unconscious. This 'information' is further clouded by our emotions and habits. But on the basis of our interpretation we act in the world at large, and in our businesses.

We act and sometimes it works out fine and sometimes it's a disaster, but we always find an explanation to suit the outcome in the firm belief that we are in control. After all, if we aren't in control, who is? Well, one thing's for sure: we can certainly act in the world and cause trouble accordingly!

No matter what our ideas about life may be, you can see that the way to act is to have advantage of as much information as possible. This is NOT the case when we intellectualise because we are only using a small subset of the information available.

After the 2004 tsunami, there were many tales of animals inexplicably fleeing to higher ground and escaping its worst ravages – all without the advantage of modern technology and weather forecasting systems. Animals are instinctual and were able to pick up information that was available to everyone – except they were listening – they had no choice.

Suspension of Belief

As part of the narrative fantasy we build a story about who we are, what we want, how things work. What is right or wrong, good or bad. We are puzzled or angry when someone has a different opinion or value system.

Exercise #1:

As an experiment, observe yourself in action. See how your mood changes when you are with someone new, someone you dislike or like, someone who can give you something or that you want.

Watch how you attribute bad motivation to a competitor. Consider how your emotion is stirred when you are falling behind on budget – or ahead.

Where is the pride or fear coming from? Is it from the situation itself or because of some conditioning from a past event?

Exercise #2:

Now imagine a stressful situation and see how the heart races, or think of a loved one and feel the calmness. But nothing has happened! The mind has triggered a response just from the thought.

So everything that happens in our minds is occurring because of how we interpret our thoughts.

When we are faced with an actual external event we have the chance to see it purely for about 90 seconds. This is our opportunity to observe our feelings dispassionately, to 'be' with them and to see them dissipate. After that golden opportunity the mind kicks in, builds a story around what has happened and triggers an emotion. If there is a strong emotion an existing habit will be strengthened or a new one established.

It took me many years to realise that I was conditioned and then be prepared to let go of some of my assumptions and beliefs. To let go of them all would be true free will – but most of us can only release a subset of our belief systems.

Nevertheless, the more we can accept and refrain from judging the more we will be open to our inner voice, which will be able to make itself heard above the din. Being attuned means dropping all our judgements and preconceptions, and to accept things as they are and without interpretation.

Leave preconceptions at the door

None of the attunement disciplines discussed here require belief. If you experiment with a method that does not deliver what it claims, then let it go – but at least give it a try. Don't get hung up with the narrative, which only serves the mind.

It doesn't matter if you agree with the narrative or not – you use a light bulb without necessarily understanding how electricity works. And most people have a problem accepting many of the basic precepts of relativity theory. For instance, things near the ground age differently to tall things. It's a minute difference and its been proven, but do you really believe that in your heart? And that's just one of the many baffling consequences of Einstein's Laws.

Those familiar with debating will also know that for every argument there is a counter-argument. Therefore, the theory of a technique is interesting, but ultimately not very helpful and possibly confusing. The only thing that matters is Does It Work?

Lastly, not every technique can be learnt from a book. For example, Transcendental Meditation is the meditation technique I use, but it has to be taught – although I can and do describe the principles herein. Other meditation methods are described in various books and you are welcome to try them, but I will only be talking from my personal experience.

Neuro-Linguistic Programming (NLP)

In the current age of spin that we inhabit, we shy away from being open and straightforward. 'Letting go' replaces 'firing' and 'pushback' replaces a plain 'no'. But how we speak mirrors how we think. If we don't communicate clearly, then we'll get confusing results and that's exactly what we have today.

In order to explore my own inconsistencies and to be able to help others, I qualified as a Neuro-Linguistic Programming Practitioner. NLP was developed in the 1960s by John Grinder and Richard Bandler.

NLP University, based in California is one of the leading NLP training facilities. As their website says:

'Neuro-Linguistic Programming describes the fundamental dynamics between mind (neuro) and language (linguistic) and how their interplay affects our body and behavior (programming).'

To put this in perspective, listen carefully to what you say and think. Note whenever you hear 'I could never do that,' or when you make an assumption like, 'Smith would never do that.' Do the same when listening to those around you. How people use language tells you a significant amount about how they see their world and the constraints they place on themselves. It tells you about what programs they have running in their nervous system that are affecting their behaviour.

NLP is also about recognising imprints and providing tools to change them. When training in NLP over the Christmas period a few years ago I went to the local Starbucks in order to buy a mince pie. There was only one mince pie left and just as I was getting to the front of the queue, the Italian tourist ahead of me bought it. I felt really disappointed – but hey it was only a mince pie.

The next day after a really heavy lunch I went back to Starbucks for a cup of tea. There was now a huge mound of mince pies and a voice inside me said: 'Mince pie – gimme one!' However, my stomach was completely full and couldn't possibly handle any more food. Nevertheless the 'mince pie' program had been set running and had not been switched off. This was about mince pies, but imagine how many other programs are still running inappropriately in your own nervous system.

NLP is a model. Its philosophy is not and does not claim to be 'truth'. Its techniques seem to help people and I offer a couple of NLP approaches below, which you might find helpful in addressing your own challenges.

NLP grew out of gestalt therapy and began by modelling excellence, or the 'difference that makes the difference.' The theory was that if you studied someone who was excellent in a skill and copied their behaviour as carefully as possible, then it would lend important insights that someone could use for their own development, not only in that field but throughout their life in general.

However, NLP has now morphed into a body of techniques which can modify the subjective experience. It does not postulate objective truth, but merely accepts that every truth is subjective and personal. A complete review of NLP is outside the scope of this book, but to give you a flavour, here are two NLP related exercises:

Exercise #1: Timelines

This exercise is best done initially with an experienced NLP practitioner – but you can try it on your own too, with positive results.

First, let me introduce you to the subject of timelines. Think of the past and locate it physically. Now think of the future. Many people think of the future as ahead of them and the past behind them, but if you have a different perception then adapt this exercise to reflect your reality.

Now imagine the timeline as an imaginary line on the floor.

Let's say you found yourself having powerful negative emotions in a meeting. When you're alone imagine the meeting again and relive it totally as if you were there.

Now with the feeling there walk backwards on your timeline, starting at the present moment, backwards towards your birth, and innocently notice as you do this, any memories that come up, until the emotion resonates with a certain memory or memories. Take time to pause at each memory, seeing what you learn in the process.

When you've done that step off the timeline, shake yourself (literally) out of the emotional state and look at your timeline as an impartial observer. What do you notice? What resources would the younger you have needed that would have helped him/her cope better at that time?

Now step, back on the 'now' position of the timeline and 'beam' those resources to the younger you in the first memory. Now walk back to the younger you position and accept these resources. Imagine really integrating them. Then walk from that past memory towards 'now', living your life again as if you had those resources.

Repeat this resourcing process for each memory until you're done.

Notice how the present 'you' now feels. Road-test it. Imagine again the difficult situation you experienced. Does it still resonate? If it does repeat the timeline process again and do it a couple more times until the experience has no hold on you.

Then in real life, notice how you are in similar situations. You will notice that you are much calmer, because you are no longer prone to the same conditioned response.

Exercise #2: Meta-mirror

Think of a situation where someone at work has really annoyed you. Now put yourself in their shoes. Really imagine being them. Make your body mirror what they do.

Now imagine being them, looking at you. Relive the annoying situation but this time from their situation. What do you learn? Give yourself time for quiet reflection.

Now relive it again, but this time as a fly on the wall. Watch the situation impartially. What advice would you give 'you' as a friend to help deal with the situation better?

Now step back into the original drama as you (in NLP – first position), but take on board what you've learnt and the friendly advice. How does it go? Take the position of the other person again (second position) and see what you learn. Now become the fly on the wall observer (third position).

And finally look at the situation again from your own vantage point (first position).

You should learn an awful lot and be able to deal with this and other situations like it much more elegantly in the future because you have opened up your awareness to a much wider range of dynamics then you first appreciated.

The benefit of seeing a situation from the others' perspective is that it will bring you to a closer understanding of their point of view, rather than accepting the belief that you are in the right and they are at best misguided.

And is that person still annoying, or do you now see them in a different, more positive light?

The Cycles of Evolution

NLP is a very modern discipline for attunement, but ancient traditions also apply to business; so some context will be helpful to those readers that may be unfamiliar with them.

Many ancient traditions say that humanity is evolving in sophistication directly in proportion to the passage of time. This assumption does not explain the remarkable archaeological feats of Mayan cities and the pyramids, but it does highlight the natural evolution of things towards unity, or growth. Eastern philosophies speak of cycles of sophistication (or raised consciousness) followed by declines. This knowledge has been preserved to various degrees in its purity, but the essence of yoga, (including meditation), is a sophisticated system that is able to maintain perfect health (without side-effects) and which understands the working of the conscious and unconscious mind as it brings them into balance.

Despite (or as well as) having a scientific background, I have always been fascinated by ancient wisdom, because it intuitively felt more holistic, than the rather disjointed approach of 'modern' technology. For instance: modern medicine tends to treat symptoms rather than causes; industrialisation uses the planet as an asset to be monetised; and technology is gross and polluting, etc.

I have no hesitation incorporating traditional practices and innovations into my spiritual and business lives – providing they work. Here I must stress again that not every method will necessarily work for you. We are all different and although I can discuss the goal of attunement, it is for you to be open to experimentation and to utilise the method that resonates with you.

Thoughts, Chance, Coincidence and Omens

Before discussing meditation, which is essentially the science of the thinking process, I want to consider the origin of thoughts. Consider where a thought comes from. You will soon realise that a thought is always generated by either another thought or an outside event.

When I was in Mumbai, I would try and visit Ramesh Balsekar, who passed away as this book was approaching publication. He was an enlightened soul and an ex-banker, who held a daily discourse for any visitors at his apartment. By enlightened, I mean that he had attained a state whereby he no longer felt himself as separate from the creation, but a part of it. This state is considered the birthright of every human in Eastern traditions.

Enlightenment is not a philosophical idea or belief but a state that is experienced by many people all over the world. The goal of attunement is to bring us closer to that state.

Ramesh always challenged his guests to find any thought they have had that they can clearly call their own. For example, you might want a cup of coffee, but the impulse for that thought comes from outside the conscious mind. Similarly, the inspiration for your holiday may come from your partner, but if you originate it, you will notice the impulse comes from 'elsewhere.' This is an extremely important point, because we have to consider where this elsewhere actually is. The answer is that the impulse will either be a habitual response from the unconscious or from the field of evolution.

Nassim Taleb, a former trader and currently a philosopher, writes in his book, *The Black Swan* about the inability of economic models to accurately predict (almost) anything. Strangely, his previous title, *Fooled by Randomness*, discussed the possibility of a plane crashing into his office building. The book was published a week before September 11, 2001. Since the whole point of his book was that unlikely events are unpredictable, he couldn't possibly believe that his musing about the plane crash was anything other than a 'coincidence.' He writes, 'it was a chance occurrence. I am not playing oracle!'

Of course he wasn't playing the oracle, but one has to also consider how that particular thought emanated. Where did this thought come from, why this particular thought and why did it arise? The fact is that the field of attunement is beyond time and space and when we are attuned we will experience insights about ourselves, about market conditions, in fact, about anything…

As I stated earlier, relativity theory postulates that time and space are interchangeable but most of us are confused in that we feel that such a concept must be irrational, whilst still accepting it to be true. As Einstein said, 'If God has created the world, his primary worry was not to make its understanding easy for us!' If we are truly rational then we must also accept that the world is a very strange place, but few of us are prepared to lay down our belief systems in the process.

When I ran my own business, I was besieged by coincidences, omens and intuitions, which my poor staff simply had to blindly obey. I would 'know' that a contract was up for grabs, that we were in danger of losing a major deal and how to resurrect discussions. For example, I could see (and I mean clearly see in my mind's eye) that premium rate phone services would become a major revenue stream for newspapers and publishers and as I have already mentioned I saw the sale of my business to News Corporation.

But when you are no longer in control of your own business destiny, then these insights become almost a hindrance because your colleagues will need a narrative or an intellectual argument.

Market trends and fashions are simply beyond traditional thinking.

Newton's Third Law of Motion states: 'For every action, there is an equal and opposite reaction.' My experience is that this Law can be applied in a far greater arena. For every idea, there will be proof and counterproof – therefore any idea is valid. It merely depends on the beliefs of its proponents.

If we simply observe our inner feelings, our path in life and business will be lit up like a highway at night.

Meditation and Yoga

Two powerful tools to enhance attunement are yoga and meditation, and either will significantly contribute to a sense of connection.

Technically, meditation is a 'limb' of yoga and the postures that most Western people think of as yoga are yet another limb. The goal of yoga with its eight limbs is to quieten the mind so that feeling of direct connection is a reality 24/7.

Any of us can experience the mind being calm, even in the midst of a heated argument about budgeting.

There are many yoga traditions and all are about bringing flexibility to the body and mind. It is not about straining the body to achieve any particular position. I strongly recommend tuition, at least for long enough to ensure that your yoga practice is safe and suitable for your body type and in the case of meditation, that you are practising correctly.

The benefits of meditation have long been advocated by corporations in Asia, and I was pleased to see recently that a number of companies like Apple, Google and Yahoo have made meditation available to their employees.

I mentioned earlier that normally the conscious mind is only able to process a relatively small amount of information when compared to the unconscious. However, regular practice facilitates an integration of mental functions, and increases the conscious faculties. It also allows a more direct intuitive contact with the evolutionary flow. Consequently, we feel more purposeful and have a better understanding of what is right for us.

Above all though, meditation or yoga have to be practiced – and regularly.

I emphasise this because although in my experience of teaching meditation I have seen that it works for almost everyone (and we're talking 90%), there are those who simply cannot sit still (although there are walking meditations). And there are others who are unable to be innocent – that is to accept whatever is happening in their meditation as correct meditation. And in yoga, some people are injuring themselves because of insufficient supervision or straining.

We can be content with knowing that our conscious mind is growing in its capacity to be rational and open to intuition.

Transcendental Meditation (TM)

As I have practiced Transcendental Meditation (TM) for over 30 years and also qualified as a TM teacher – this was the course where I had my business 'calling' – I will discuss the principles of this technique. Again, I am not claiming it is better than other meditation techniques – it just worked for me.

TM works by silently repeating a meaningless (in English!) Sanskrit sound – a *mantra* – in such way that the mind naturally dives into calmer and finer thinking 'levels', until a state is reached which feels pleasant and expanded, and momentarily (at first) there is direct connection with the whole consciousness, which is beyond thoughts and meaning.

Continued practice of the technique produces calmness even in the midst of hectic activity and there are a number of other benefits, including a drop in blood pressure and heightened visual perception. Also, the momentary connection to evolution becomes longer and remains in activity.

I started TM at university convinced it was a con and determined to expose it. I was searching for a method that would help me dissolve stress, having almost flunked my first year due to nerves. TM worked alarmingly well for me. So much so that my final results were contested by my tutor, who didn't believe I was capable of such high grades (Proof of the maxim, 'First impressions are last impressions!').

But as I stressed above, it may not suit everyone. TM doesn't work by itself – you have to find regular slots to practice. And some people can't believe it's so easy and they begin to strain. But almost every one of my friends who practices it reports that the results are quite remarkable.

Here are a couple of quotes from the TM in business website (www.tmbusiness.org/endorsements) that illustrate the benefits of TM in a business setting:

'TM has made a big difference, both at work or at home. I'm able to stay focused—see the big picture and attend to the specific issues that need immediate attention. Meditating has definitely made my life more enjoyable and more successful.'

Martha Zimmerman attorney at law, litigator; Chadwick

'I have spent most of my career in the auto industry—and that's a fairly high-stressed way to make a living—especially these days. The stakes are enormous. The pressure to win is constant. The need for creativity is critical. The relationships with hundreds of people and the way you handle those relationships and the individuals you're dealing with – they all impact your success rate. Your mind is turning over all the time. You constantly have to fill it up and then clear it off for the next subject, fill it and clear it off. I think pretty much all business is like that. For me Transcendental Meditation provides the clearing off or cleansing. It's like taking a bucket of water, throwing it on your dirty car, and watching the dirt wash off until you have a nice, shiny car again. TM didn't impact my religious beliefs or any other beliefs. It didn't get in the way of anything. It didn't take a degree in nuclear physics to understand. It was just a very simple, relaxing technique that gave my brain a chance to breathe at the beginning and end of each work day. And that was a tremendous help to me.'

Bud Liebler, principal, Liebler!MacDonald

In business, meditation has been helpful to me in that even in a 'crisis' like the current credit crunch, I am able to function and not get caught up too much in the drama. I will always remember a business rival calling me 'laid back', which was the ultimate compliment, since before taking up TM, I was a nervous wreck!

Breathing

Next time you are fortunate enough to be in the presence of a baby, do yourself a favour and notice how it breathes. You'll see that every healthy baby breathes regularly, without holding, and the breath will flow into its abdomen.

Now take a moment and discover how you breathe. Put one hand on your chest and another on your stomach and observe your breath. Does the breath seem to emanate from your chest or stomach? Is it shallow or full, smooth or erratic? Do you find yourself holding your breath and then taking a sudden sharp intake?

Soon after we are born we begin to take on the stress of the world about us, and this is embedded into our breathing pattern and becomes habitual. Most of us in the West have shallow, chest breathing. This is the breathing pattern of stress, contributing to hypertension and a compromised immune system. I only learnt about the importance of breathing recently because my partner specialises in breath work, but I can testify to the transformative effects that can be achieved simply by taking deeper breaths and noticing any holding patterns.

Again, while to get the best results it's good to have a teacher, either in breath work or singing – there are still a number of simple things you can do at home or at the office. What is more, the beauty of these techniques is that you can do them in the midst of a meeting without anyone noticing!

Exercise #1:

Firstly, practice taking deep, natural, regular breaths. It is important NOT to try. Simply put your hand on your stomach and get used to the air flowing fully into your lungs. If you get the chance, look at an anatomy book and see how large your lungs actually are. Now you will understand that by only taking shallow chest breaths, you are not giving your body sufficient oxygen and it will strain as a result.

Next notice, how it is unnecessary to make an effort to breathe in and then breath out. It happens by itself with no effort.

The lungs are a bridge between the conscious and unconscious mind. The heart beats by itself automatically and the breath breathes by itself! But, uniquely (well almost – see below), the breath can also be consciously controlled. We can hold our breath or deliberately take a deep breath.

This realisation was of major significance to yogis in India because they realised that this was the key to gaining mastery of every aspect of their nervous systems. Even today yogis can be found who can control all of their 'automatic' functions. They can make their heart stop or go without breath (or sometimes food) for long periods. They have integrated their conscious and unconscious, which is the goal of all these techniques.

For us, once we realise that our breath reflects our state of being we are in a position to take control and ensure we are functioning at our peak.

The breath is our link to the outer world. We literally breathe it in. When we are distrustful we also breathe shallowly, whereas when we are open to life our breath is full and rich.

Once you have mastered the art of breathing naturally, it will become a habit and can be used as a simple meditation technique whenever and wherever we are: in the boardroom, on the phone, or travelling to work, for instance. Simply put attention on your breath, watch it ebb and flow and you will be surprised at how effective this procedure is at grounding the mind and enabling you to make better judgements.

Exercise #2:

As a further experiment, notice how you breathe when you are with your partner, friends, or when you see someone you like or dislike, or when you are under strain or running for a bus, or running for pleasure.

Next time you are feeling tense take steady, deep breaths and you will inevitably notice a relaxation. Don't gasp, just allow the breath to flow deeply into your lungs and then release and fully exhale.

With simple observation, you will become adept at recognising when you have 'lost your breath', in the sense that you are not giving the body the oxygen it needs to function at peak efficiency.

Now let's assume you have put some of these techniques into practice. What difference will they make to your everyday business life? You will appreciate the benefit of incorporating mental silence into your routine on a regular basis, and of the sense of calm and centredness that breathing gives to your body and mind.

Intention

Subtle intention is the term I use to describe the way you can ensure you will reach your goal. It's a knowingness of your destiny.

When you have cleared your inner tensions and seen through some of your habitual conditioning, then you will have a much better idea of your destiny. Therefore, there is no need to strain on the outcome.

This is fundamentally different from a visualization technique, which would have you imagining the outcome, seeing the profit figures, hearing the praise from colleagues and smelling the success. It is different in that this vision will come to you spontaneously – if it is your destiny – and if your way of attuning is a visual one.

We all have different ways of interpreting our future, with the visual and auditory fields predominating, but how intuition manifests is different for every one of us. And what if you don't have an intuitive knowledge of your path? Then ask yourself some questions along the lines of: 'How can I best be of service to my company?' or 'How can I best make budget?' Ask and let go. This does not mean laying awake at night and churning over your problems. In fact, from the viewpoint of attunement, this is the worst thing you can do!

When you practice any of the techniques above, you will soon reach the state of inner calmness from which you divine a workable strategy.

For instance: my office used to be near a canal, and whenever I had what seemed to be an insurmountable problem, I would walk along it alone, or even take one of my team with me. It was extraordinary how we would inevitably come up with a creative response.

Compare this with the workaholic mentality we see all around us today, where employees are so exhausted all their creative juices have been dissipated, yet it is considered macho to be at the office at all hours – despite the wonders of new technology.

My company was a round-the-clock operation, but whenever I saw an employee overwhelmed by a problem at the office, I sent them off to have some fun and to return when they were rested, either with a solution, or in a state to solve it with myself, or our team.

I have mentioned several times how I eventually lost my way in business, but when we began and were on track, we had over 90% of the UK premium rate business in our sector and we were having enormous fun winning contract after contract.

Once you know what you are there to do, then you have to set intent. Just direct your subconscious to achieve the goal. If all parts of you are integrated and working together then your subconscious will know exactly what to do, it won't be hearing mixed messages and it will drive you forward with the minimum effort.

By the way, I have not mentioned prayer in this section, but if prayer comes naturally to you, then a meditative contemplation can be termed the subtle intention I am advocating.

Letting Go

You'll also notice I use the words 'let go' above. This is the second part of the key of intent (and runs counter to most team building exercises!). For intent to be the most powerful, you cannot be attached to the outcome. I appreciate this is difficult to accept, especially for those of us who have been brought up in competitive environments, but if something is our true destiny, then it will manifest.

As the proverb goes, 'Beware of what you wish for!'

If we are not attuned then what we want does not necessarily accord with our destiny, but because we have free will, we can still make it happen, albeit with evolution kicking and screaming against us! If we are attuned however, we will experience a flow going with our actions and even when things don't seem to get where we thought they would, there is a feeling of 'rightness' about the outcome.

Now you're aligned

Once we understand what our goal is and every cell in our body is 'on message', it is time for the maximum application of focus and energy.

It is important to realise that destiny is time specific. Which means that the 'right' action has a sell-by date. This may be a few hours, minutes, days or months away – but it is there and therefore if we do not act then the desirable goal might have changed, without us realising. This is self-evident when we consider the ebbs and flows of market conditions, but it is surprising how often this simple fact is forgotten in businesses.

Curiously, when you are attuned, motivation comes simply from knowing you're fulfilling the actions required of you. In a way, the goal is immaterial. And a by-product is that you will have the energy to achieve your goal and feel enlivened getting there. Focus on the road ahead, avoid the many distractions you will find on the way, including pessimism from the 'can't doers', idle gossip (which is draining) and the myriad of other distractions that will come your way to take you off your path.

For maximum energy it is necessary to live a balanced life with plenty of fun and time for friends and family. When you are attuned, your project or business will enhance the lives of those around you and you will know that your actions have a beneficial influence beyond your wildest expectations.

Intention, Focus, Motivation and Energy: these four factors hold the key to the execution of a successful spiritual business life. Once you are aligned you are on the way to living your true purpose – and in these rapidly changing times that can be easier said than done, I know.

In conclusion, there is no substitute for 'being'. We have no hesitation in launching ourselves into our next business project, but when it comes to self-development we remain rather coy.

I invite you to try the ideas above and to find new ones. Caring for your inner state will enable you to become more intuitive, calmer and able to tune in to yourself and those around you.

WORKBOOK:

To achieve maximum success in business there are a number of modalities that can increase your awareness and effectiveness, including breathing, meditation, NLP and others. What I'd like you to do now is list as many modalities as you currently use to help you in your business life, and describe how they help you.

_____

_____

_____

_____

_____

_____

_____

_____

To enable the unconscious and conscious mind to work together it is necessary to set intent. List not only some examples of when you have had a focused intent, but how that has helped anchor and manifest your desired outcome.

_____

_____

_____

_____

_____

_____

_____

_____

The unconscious wants to please but needs to be programmed by the conscious mind. Our nervous system provides a direct connection to the evolutionary flow – we need only listen to the inner voice, to see omens as expressions of the outer voice and to act decisively and in a timely manner. List some examples of your inner voice, or of outer omens that have affected your actions in your business dealings.

_____

_____

_____

_____

_____

_____

_____

_____

Chapter 5

Money is Energy

He that is of the opinion money will do everything may well be suspected of doing everything for money.

Benjamin Franklin

Despite what you hear, the current global financial crisis has not been caused by bankers, or toxic debt, or multinationals. These are only the symptoms. The ultimate cause is in *human nature* itself.

Our human condition is played out on a vast canvas where we can live out our dreams and nightmares. One of our most cherished games is that of business and its driver is money – and it is fast becoming apparent that money is an elaborate confidence trick held up by an entrenched belief system, which is becoming evermore unsteady.

Early money systems used rice, dogs' teeth, beads and many other symbols to carry out the bartering process. Then bartering was replaced by totems representing a 'value' respected across cultures. Often this was gold, a metal imbued with artificial worth. At one point most currencies could be converted to gold at a pre-set rate and consequently trading was possible between different cultures (it beats paying your suppliers with a combination of beads and spices).

As I mentioned earlier in this book, business is about creating something of 'value' and selling to a customer so that there is mutual fulfillment in the transaction.

However if you begin to believe that accumulating money leads to happiness you are in trouble, because getting a big bonus, or accumulating assets doesn't lead to more than fleeting satisfaction. You therefore believe that more money might just do the job! So bankers get bigger bonuses in a futile attempt to feel happy in themselves.

There was a time when I believed this too. First I thought if I had a £1 million in the bank and an annual income of £200k I'd have made it. But then when I 'achieved' that and my kids were going to an expensive school, and I had a gigantic mortgage and interest rates were rising, and all my peers had bigger houses, I revised the figures upwards. *Ultimately there is no figure that brings peace of mind.*

Luckily, I realised that instead of always struggling for more, I could be perfectly happy on less and I radically downsized. Now I have enough money to work when I want and to travel whenever I feel like it. This was the freedom I'd been searching for.

The irony is that many people think I'm far richer than I actually am. They cannot understand how I can support my lifestyle without having millions stashed away in some offshore bank account. But when I explain that it's simply a question of downsizing and not compromising my values for work, they nod their heads in disbelief and begin to give me excuses for why they're still pressuring themselves to 'achieve'.

Normally these excuses focus on the need to support themselves or their family in the future. They have a constructed a foolproof defence of their struggling which, of course, I am not in a position to judge. One friend cannot retire, he tells me, because he wants to be able to support his (yet unborn) grandchildren – a completely rock solid excuse!

There is nothing inherently wrong with having wealth or working hard if it is enjoyed and shared. But when we are toiling away and taking ten days vacation (if that) a year and when we rate people highly because they are well-known, and look down on others, then something is awry with our own value system, and it is a long way from the enlightened ideals we have discussed in the previous chapters.

The enlightened approach to business is to either use money, or give it away.

Either give excess capital back to shareholders, or to charity. But first you must ensure prices are fair, and that suppliers and employees are adequately compensated no matter where they are based. Of course, any business has to plan for the future and allow sufficient funds for contingencies, but money sitting in a bank account that will never be used acquires toxicity. And this applies both personally and in companies.

This may be a radical idea in today's age of investment capitalism, but it starts from a holistic foundation that recognises that money and business are two separate entities.

Yet money and business are so intrinsically entwined nowadays that you could say the two are held together by an umbilical cord. Business today means maximising profit, which equates to making money, but that hasn't always been the case. And as the global financial system gets a much needed overhaul, we now need to place business back within a broader framework.

Our life consists of friends, family, sunshine, laughter, food, breathing, walking, swimming, dancing, sadness, health and illness, to name just a handful of things. Money is something that can fuel our ability to do and enjoy certain activities, but it doesn't automatically create a better life for us. Yet in business we focus almost exclusively on making money and we fail to give context to the role of business in our wider lives, or what money is supposed to do for us.

The Secret of Money
There are many books that have been written about how we can make more cash and 'succeed', how to be wealthy and live the lifestyle of the rich and

famous. These books distort the true role of money in a rich and success-ful life and create an impossible objective for culture as a whole. Celebrities are valued more than nurses and CEO's often earn millions of dollars more than their humblest employee. And all this is considered normal and natural – and then we wonder why our working life is full of stress!

Advertising works to make us continually want more. If we could just stop for a moment and pass through the inner chatter to our own security, we'd see that everything we need is with us right now – it's only our men-tal attitude that needs adjusting.

There was a time not too long ago when people would go to the cinema or a theatre show, suspend judgement for a few hours and get caught up in the drama, have a good laugh or cry, then come back to their 'real' lives. Now the 'show' is everywhere we look – the illusion we have created has overtaken the reality – and very few of us even realise it. We're too busy scrabbling to climb the corporate ladder, or just making ends meet to question the treadmill we're on, or to ask where it's taking us. And money is what powers that treadmill.

Not that things are any different in the secularised Eastern countries. Upper class Indian families are now emulating their Western counterparts and treating their servants with disdain. The situation there is made all the worse by the belief that the lower castes have bad karma and deserve what they get. Money has become a cultural weapon to control those with it, as much as those without it, but that's not what money truly is.

So what *is* money, then? I hear you ask. If money is so ephemeral, what is it? *It's a form of energy.*

How can this be? Scientists agree that the building blocks of the uni-verse are pure energy and that matter is a manifestation of energy. Einstein's famous equation $E = mc^2$ states that in any mass the amount of energy contained is enormous. This understanding laid the foundation for both unlimited energy from nuclear power and the atomic bomb.

If energy is the building block of the universe, then it follows that every-thing in the universe has at its basis, energy. This applies equally, if surpris-ingly, to thoughts and consciousness and more obviously to money.

It is the nature of energy that it needs to flow and create. Thoughts flow to create ideas in our consciousness. And from ideas we construct our environment and our relationships. Similarly, money flows into business dealings, which in turn become new buildings, restaurants, furniture and call centres, etc.

Destiny calls us to act. It demands that we follow through on our ideas – otherwise we become frustrated. It asks that we make our money work for us, otherwise it becomes a noose round our necks.

Similarly, having money in the bank as 'potential energy' may temporarily make us feel secure, but it's only when it flows that it can achieve something worthwhile in the world. So we have to change our focus from accumulation and instead consider how we can move money around and utilise funds for employing more people, developing products and opening new markets.

It's quite likely that you, like most business people, have been doing the right things, but you may not have been thinking about them in the most effective way. Doing a big deal should not only be about collecting a large fee so you can buy a second home in the Berkshires. It should at heart be around the genuine desire to create an expansive feeling of connection in ourselves and others. Because *how* we make money is fundamental to consequences that will be produced.

The trouble with having 'too much' is that it encourages inertia. The attention can turn from utilising capital to fearing its decimation; from being open-minded to being prisoners of capitalism. Happy rich business people hate money sitting around in their bank account. They increasingly look at giving it away through charitable trusts. Bill Gates, Warren Buffett, Michael Bloomberg and many others have led by example as they attempt to make the money they have accumulated work for the good of humankind.

From the enlightened standpoint the degree to which we can put money to work, the greater its capacity to fulfill us, and those around us.

If we see money as an energy that is meant to naturally flow through us, then holding on to it will, conversely, create stress. I am infinitely richer than the 1.6 billion people living below the poverty line. And the wealthiest folk on this planet are infinitely richer than me. But that does not absolve me from ensuring that I take an appropriate level of responsibility for distributing some of what I have to those less fortunate.

Giving It Back

This is embodied in an old practice called 'tithing', which says that you give a portion of your overall income, say 10 percent, to feed those who have spiritually fed you. This may mean donating to a charity, an individual, or an organisation that you feel is doing good in the world and that you wish to support.

Many religions speak of the evils of money and certainly it can lead people astray and into a poverty of emotion. Many traditions insist that to attain a balanced perspective on life the individual must spend a time as a *sadhu,* monk, or penitent, living at the mercy of the elements and the charity of householders.

I have a business friend who regularly embarks on a 'pilgrimage' with just a passport and change of clothes. He sets himself ambitious goals to reach overseas retreats and the like overland, trusting fate to see him there in good form. Along the journey he always has 'rich' experiences of life that he would never encounter in his business world, and he is also charmed by the generosity of strangers who are only too eager to share their meager belongings.

Such experiences enable us to appreciate that happiness is not related to the accumulation of money itself.

Charity is one of the most effective means of gaining fulfillment, and the highest form of charity is anonymous. This is particularly challenging for ego-bound business people who want to leave a legacy. After all, how can you leave a legacy if nobody knows you left it? I am sure there are examples of the anonymously funded hospital, but more often the benefactor is named. Realistically, though, any charity is better than nothing.

We can easily see how an individual can distribute a certain proportion of their wealth to 'good works', but a company will still have the inevitable conflict between safeguarding the interests of its shareholders in financial terms and satisfying the goals of its Board, who might want to do some good in the outside world.

The more these two drivers are aligned, however, the more effective enlightened businesspeople we become, both as individuals and as companies. And there is growing evidence in the business world that this awareness of mutual sustainability is on the rise.

The odds are that if you're reading this book you may have become uncomfortable with the single-mindedness of the money-based value system around us. Or you may think it's fine, but want some deeper understanding of *why* it is like it is. Whichever the case, the ideas presented here will help you see your relationship to money in a more holistic way, and facilitate a healthy balance that is fundamental to becoming an enlightened business person.

First let us acquire humility, gratitude and equanimity about what we have and what we have achieved. Nearly all the time in business is spent worrying about the future. How can I become wealthy? How can my business succeed? How can I gain the respect of my peers? We imagine doing a bigger deal, buying our larger competitor, owning a yacht or plane, etc. Living the dream.

So just for once try an experiment: Review your business achievements and also your circumstances. Mentally retrace your footsteps, looking at all the success you have had over the years, all those milestones. Remember the best deal you have done and relive that feeling of satisfaction. Perhaps you feel you are not successful – yet? Is that true? Look back honestly at the moments when you felt you'd made progress of some kind. Let that feeling fully immerse you as if it were happening again right now. It feels good, right?

Now imagine that you have enough and that everything is just right and just as it should be. You will probably feel expansive and ready for action, with an easing of the continual tension that is associated with the feeling of lack so often evident in corporations. This is the state you are striving for, isn't it? You imagine that by achieving your goals this state will happen automatically in the future, but in actuality it's here right now: as you read this book, or walk down the street, as you go to bed or sit in a budget meeting.

So What's All The Fuss About?

Business is both a creative expression and the fulfillment of our destiny. But it is the *process* of business that is rewarding. Accumulation of money for its own sake merely creates fear. And the most effective state to be in when doing business is one of non-attachment.

This of course, runs counter to the obsessive and illusory business culture we live in, where struggle and competitiveness are the bywords. Therefore it is essential to remind ourselves at regular intervals that it's not about the money. Indeed, as we discussed above, many of the richest and most creative businesspeople give much of their accumulated wealth away so that it can do more good than clogging up their bank account.

Let's now look at the various ways in which the obsession with money for it's own sake has corrupted our values, so that we can at least attempt to balance out anomalies in our own enterprises.

Affluenza

Trading must be undertaken with compassion and respect, so that both parties gain. But this can only happen when people are comfortable in themselves and do not look outside to their peers for a feeling of self-worth. Sadly, these days we have gone to the extreme opposite of self-referral, with society obsessed with looking outwards for self-validation. For example, in *USA Today* (Jan 9, 2007) I saw this report:

'Eighty-one percent of 18 to 25-year-olds surveyed in a Pew Research Center poll released today said getting rich is their generation's most important or second-most-important life goal; 51% said the same about being famous.'

'We're seeing the common person become famous for being themselves,' says David Morrison of the Philadelphia-based research firm Twentysomething Inc. 'MTV and reality TV are in large part fueling these youthful desires,' he says.

'Look at Big Brother and other shows. People being themselves can be incredibly famous and get sponsorship deals, and they can become celebrities,' he says. 'It's a completely new development in entertainment, and it's having a crossover effect on attitudes and behavior.'

Previous generations wanted to make a contribution to society, with fame being a by-product but the present obsession with money and fame, have produced a sickness and a loss of balanced values.

The psychologist Oliver James, in his book of the same name, calls it *Affluenza*: where there is a complete disconnection from the world around and where people become Marketing Characters (a term coined by Erich Fromm), whom James describes as those who 'experience themselves as commodities whose value and meaning are externally determined.'

Once again, the sheer unreality of this is currently not seen through because of low levels of consciousness. And those that achieve money and fame are faced with a corresponding spiritual void, which many increasingly fill with drugs.

Instead we need 'self referral', whereby our frame of reference is our true nature and we experience being part of the universal flow.

Shopping as Religion

On the Sundays of my childhood, when the church and shop unions were more powerful, London used to come to a complete standstill. Now Sunday is the major revenue generator for most stores. Shopping has replaced religion as the central leisure activity of the masses and shopping malls are the new churches. Money is the new God.

The Apple store in Regent's Street, London (which I love) is another case in point. It's housed in a beautiful, old refurbished building with an enormous staircase leading upwards. The sales assistants are all dressed in black and the store itself is apparently empty of product. You have to look very carefully from outside to spot the cabinets of iPods and iPhones and Apple Macs. I have no doubt that a marketing genius somewhere planned a visit to this Apple store as a religious experience.

But it's not just the Apple brand – the 'original sin' goes a lot deeper, and money itself has been called 'the root of all evil'. With material wealth having so many emotional hooks, it's no wonder that many of us fall into the honey trap and believe that owning a new car, computer, phone, etc., will make us feel better.

But being 'rich' means having abundance on all levels. And abundance is that simple feeling of fulfillment or satisfaction that money can't buy. To illustrate this point let me quote from the British philosopher Peter Russell, who poses two simple questions, which highlight the transient satisfaction of shopping:

1. If I have that ... (car, dress, house, corporate jet etc.) how long will I be happy for?

The answer is invariably 'not long'.

2. If I don't have that ... (car, dress, house, corporate jet etc.) can I still be happy?

And of course, everyone realises that yes, happiness is still absolutely possible.

Nevertheless, because we have a taste of happiness we begin to imagine that having more material possessions will lead to a *permanent* state of fulfillment. And this mistake is the driving force behind our need for money.

There is nothing inherently 'wrong' in having money or wealth. Nor can I or anyone else dictate what is the 'right' amount for you, or whether you should have 200 pairs of shoes or suits, etc. The issue about material possessions is that they should not be a burden. Nor should the money that purchases them.

I struggled for decades to have the ability to treat myself occasionally. I'm having a great time now – but some of my best lessons have still been learnt despite money, not because of it. For instance:

On one occasion my partner and I traveled to India and stayed in the ashram of a spiritual teacher called Amma (The Hugging Mother). We were housed in a cell-like room and slept on a mattress on the concrete floor. Our sleep was disturbed throughout the night by chanting. Frankly, a good hotel is much more comfortable but staying in the ashram was one of the most interesting (and challenging) times I have ever experienced.

To sum it up, I believe we should always live in harmony with our material desires. They should not control us. We should enjoy what we have, and develop a habit of being grateful rather than continually scrambling for more.

The Family Business

You may have been born into 'money', or, more precisely, into the family business that makes the family money. If so, you may be familiar with the burden family money can bring, and the inherent expectations it can make of you.

In the past, family played a much stronger role in defining our careers. As I mentioned earlier, my grandfather set up a large optical business, which was destroyed in WWII. Those actions left my father and his siblings to struggle with the consequences of being brought up in a wealthy entrepreneurial family hit by disaster.

I was too young to understand these dynamics when I was growing up – but now I recognise how my father and his brother had to deal with their dilemma (there were two sisters, but in those days they were not expected to play an active role in the business).

If you have the fortune to be born into a family business, you will have to decide whether to stay within it or move away, as I did. You will have to face issues of succession and sibling rivalry, and decide to stay loyal to longstanding suppliers – who may have served your family firm for decades – or switch to a competitive newcomer.

Perhaps generations of family members have built the business from scratch and there is a chance to hand down something of value to future generations, opening up issues of legacy. The attraction of selling the business will have to be weighed against the dubious benefits of sitting on a cash pile and the related feelings of lack of purpose.

In their book *Family Wars*, authors Grant Gordon and Nigel Nicholson describe the squabbles of so many family founded businesses, such as IBM, U-Haul, Viacom and Seagram. What they reveal is that being in a powerful family business has its own hornet's nest of issues – and money is frequently equated with love and loyalty. So traditional family business is not always smooth sailing.

But whether our business comes from a bloodline or whether we are part of a large 'faceless' corporation, we will get the maximum fulfillment for ourselves and for those who come into contact with us by adopting positive family principles like loyalty, love, generosity and trust.

So often we hear corporate jargon dictating how we can improve company performance, but as with most important things in life, the principles of simplicity and compassion can guide as well. When we are with our children and friends we are more inclined to be generous with our money than when we are working in a corporation, where all sorts of other agendas seem to come into play.

Why should this be? The same people who are working in our organisations have families and of course, outside of work they may be our friends – and yet the corporation will often have a completely different set of values to our own.

Again, this is mass conditioning to the detriment of human values, which inevitably leads to dis-ease on both a personal, and collective level.

Local Money

One of the most interesting enlightened applications of money is in local initiatives.

The British Town of Lewes recently launched the largest currency in Britain for more than a century with its Lewes Pound, which can be exchanged for British pounds. The Lewes Pound can be used in 50 local shops. Meanwhile in the Southern Berkshires of Massachussetts, BerkShares is a local currency issued by BerkShares, Inc., a non-profit organisation working in collaboration with participating local banks, businesses, and NGOs.

Local Money brings together a community. Shopkeepers decide whether they want to participate in encouraging people to shop locally (discounts are often given for payment in local currency) and shoppers commit to their local retailers by converting some of their national currency into the local equivalent.

This simple system places energy back into the heart of a community and yet it is so simple. Indeed, it's just a little above bartering in its level of sophistication. It removes all the abstractions inherent in the traditional capitalist system and restores money to its natural place of facilitating local trade.

There are around 9000 local currency schemes operating around the world today. It is unrealistic to assume local currencies will catch on everywhere, but it is heartening to see that more communities are realising that ultimately trade is about improving quality of life, and that on this level it can bring personal and community fulfillment.

Money and Health

You'll recall that my journey to writing this book saw me contract and recover from cancer. The world is full of people who, with the best intentions, will try and find a reason why I fell ill. I had colon cancer, and there is allegedly a correlation with diet and stress. However at the time of my diagnosis I was a vegetarian and meditating two hours a day – so it is difficult to see how my diet and lifestyle could have been better.

However, as I mentioned in my introduction, my life had become unhappy, especially because I was anxious to adopt a more compassionate business life and I was finding myself unable to take the steps necessary. And the longer I procrastinated the weaker I became, culminating in a downwards cycle, and my eventual collapse.

Although I intuitively knew I was sick, I thought admitting it would be a sign of weakness and the sale of my business would not go through at the price I had agreed. I was playing Russian Roulette for the sake of money.

My own illness and subsequent recovery were dramatic. I certainly would not wish such experiences on anyone! But I'm stubborn and thick-skinned and I needed a near-death experience to shake me out of my bubble. When I see my peers burning the midnight oil and looking stressed, or when I hear of the corporate nonsense they put up with and the strain it puts on their loved ones, I wish I could give them a glimpse of how wonderful the world is for me, now that I can look at it from a more harmonious vantage point.

Our motivations for working hard are many and complex and, as I constantly emphasise, if hard work is fulfilling, then fantastic. We are all built differently and some of us (but not me!) have tremendous stamina and need little sleep. But we need balance and periods of rest and recuperation. And no amount of money is adequate compensation for ill health.

I recently overheard a conversation between a turn-around specialist and a friend. He was saying, almost boastfully, that the long hours involved in saving a retailing conglomerate had caused his heart condition. This is pure insanity! Our health and relationships are our most valuable possessions, so let's respect them and treat our bodies with love and compassion

– as we would like to treat others.

Money also produces stress on the emotional level. The psychologist Oliver James, in *Affluenza,* cites a World Health Organisation study which shows the United States, the world's richest nation, is the most anxious. Over 25% of its population suffered some form of depression, anxiety, substance abuse or impulsivity-aggression in the past twelve months, as opposed to Nigeria and China at under 5% and Italy at 8.2%.

Actually, it's not the money. It's the combination of wealth and culture that produces the strain. If you are always comparing yourself to others, then no amount of money can make you happy and there is the other trap of the toxicity associated with stagnant wealth.

There's nothing more guaranteed to make you happy than putting money to the service of others – not only as charity (although this is commendable) but also by becoming actively involved in helping those around you who are less fortunate.

Or you can spend all day worrying about the stock market, what others' think of you and how to hold on to what you've accumulated – a sure recipe for emotional meltdown!

Money's place in the Evolutionary Flow

As recently as 50 years ago it was possible to die from an infection due to the lack of antibiotics. One hundred years before that it was impossible to heat a house because there was no central heating and no plumbing. In a very short time this has changed and advances in medicine and technology have made our lives infinitely more comfortable.

We *should* be advancing rapidly, but the problem is that with fear mentality still so prevalent in 21st century life we tend to think of ourselves, rather than having a more expansive approach. Because money has already bought us the fundamental things we need like food and shelter, we tend to stockpile additional funds and fear losing them.

To move on as a culture we need to unravel this blockage around money by seeing it once again as the tool it is in our lives, not the outcome. This frees up the energy of money and reveals the abundance inherent in the universe as it works through us. Once we accept this, then bounty can be spread across all of humanity.

This change will not happen by wishful thinking or legislation. It requires an expansion of consciousness on the individual level which will shift the emphasis towards love, understanding and compassion. One benefit of the financial crisis is that we are experiencing a softening of our attitude to individual wealth.

Although large sections of humanity live in comfort, and even developing countries like India and China are catching up with Western standards, there are more people now living below the poverty line than ever before.

As with any paradigm shift, we have a choice as to whether we embrace it or hang on to the old ways. Those businesses that adopt a more empathic, sharing and compassionate outlook will thrive because they will be going 'with the flow' of evolution, whilst those that continue to grab as much money for themselves irrespective of ways and means, will wither.

If we adopt the enlightened attitude of non-attachment and quietly focus on our work, our ability to be 'successful' will be enhanced – in the realm of money and in the deeper realms the energy behind money springs from.

Small Change

If we are to become enlightened business people we have to transform our attitude to money so that it's in line with spiritual principles. Here are some ideas to help to accelerate this process:

- Practice Attunement (as previously discussed) and the Gratitude Exercise (that is, saying thank you for what you have received) regularly.
- Practice Non-Attachment. Give something you own away to someone who would appreciate it even more than you do. I gave my car away to a penniless student in the North of England, and my Cartier watch to one of my sons. I now wear a watch that belonged to my late grandfather, which has a sentimental rather than monetary value. We are not talking about living a life of frugality or major downsizing, but letting go of our attachments is very liberating and helps us to undestand that life can go on perfectly satisfyingly without clogging it up with stuff.
- When you think about business, focus on its non-monetary benefits as well as its monetary ones. Remember the jobs you are creating, the interesting people you have met, the adventures and fun you have had and the excitement you get from the deals – all the pluses that improve your life.
- Practice random acts of corporate kindness. Praise and empower the people you work with.
- Be truthful. Think about your actions in business and align them to those you use at home.

The healthiest attitude we can have to money is that of equanimity. We all know what business is about and the way it challenges us – but we have to put our focus on working for its own sake – as a means to fulfilling ourselves and those around us. We need to treat everyone positively and as if they were family members and be prepared to spread our wealth as extensively as we can and in a life-supporting manner.

Because if money is really energy and it comes from a universal and infinite source, then the more we let go and spread the money around, the more we sustain ourselves and those around us.

WORKBOOK:

Money is energy and should be used with an awareness of how that energy affects those around us. List some examples of how money is used in your life to fuel your dreams and everyday dealings.

_____

_____

_____

_____

_____

_____

_____

_____

Understand what it really means to be rich (abundant in all life offers). List some examples of how abundant you are in life – not just rich in a monetary sense.

_____

_____

_____

_____

_____

_____

_____

Despite popular opinion, money is not the 'root of all evil' and it can be utilised in a holistic context for the business world. Can you think of some personal examples where you, or your company has used money in an altruistic way in the community?

_____

_____

_____

_____

_____

_____

_____

In this age of virtual trading and electronic money, the context of money itself must be re-examined to better appreciate how to use it more effectively for ourselves, our clients and our shareholders. Can you list some ways that you would do this in your company?

_____

_____

_____

_____

_____

_____

_____

_____

Chapter 6

Company Consciousness

There is no life without consciousness; there is no consciousness without life.

Annie Besant

When I started my business Broadsystem, back in 1986, I wanted it to be different from any company that I previously worked for. I wanted it to be fun, innovative, creative, informal and quirky like me – 'Quirky Kirky'.

It all got off to a very promising start. I wanted the offices to be cheap, funky and near my home. I bumped into an acquaintance, Michael, at a cocktail party who owned a recording studio in Camden, one of the trendiest areas of London and just a few miles from where I was living.

He cleared out a broom cupboard so we could install our computer – which was the lifeline of the business – and found an old back office, which could house me, and the few staff I intended to recruit.

His facilities had an amazingly vibrant reception area, were open 24/7 (as Broadsystem had to be), and a café that served excellent toast and tea – my staple diet in those days! We had nothing in writing between us as we were mates and I didn't want any long-term commitment in case the business failed.

Everything went swimmingly for the first year. Clients loved coming to see 'our' offices. I kept them well away from my cubby-hole and the computer broom cupboard and met them in the café where they could ogle at the famous rock stars.

Then one day Michael called me into his office and told me that he had sold his business to a large record company and that he'd be off to live in Majorca, Spain, as a tax exile.

A couple of weeks later a new Managing Director, representing the record company, appeared on the scene and summoned me into his office. I was given a month to leave.

This could have been a death-knell to my business, which was really beginning to take off. Specifically, it would take about three months to re-house the computer. I pleaded and as a big favour the new MD allowed me to leave the computer, but he wanted me out with no access to the offices as he was tightening up security.

I wandered into the street outside to get some air and to take stock of the situation. Opposite me was an old red-brick building called The Elephant House (named, by the way, after Elephant Beer which used to be brewed there) with a 'To Let' sign. My heart skipped a beat. I ran over to the entrance and found the landlord – I'll call him Tony – sitting in a small separate outhouse on the far side of the cobbled car-park. He had the demeanor of a young Royal. He sat at the job with his feet on his desk and his black brogues reflecting the sunlight coming through the skylight.

I told him I needed space urgently and I could see his eyes light up. I only wanted a couple of small offices but he could see I was desperate and therefore he was only willing to negotiate a blanket deal on two remaining un-let floors. I wasn't in much of a position to negotiate. By that time we had loads of cash, so I could easily afford the rent, but what would I do with the space? I ensured I could sub-let all the excess capacity and walked back to the recording studios and announced to my amazed staff that we were about to be evicted but – fear not – I had already secured a new home.

One final problem remained however. How could we operate the equipment remotely? This was long before the days of networking and the only solution was to connect a cable between the two buildings – but how could we do that?

I was discussing this with Colin Turner – always a man with a plan – as we crossed the road to see the new offices. For some reason he glanced up and noticed a cable running above the street between the recording studios and The Elephant House! It transpired that it was a link between TV-AM (Bruce Gyngell's aforementioned company) and the recording studios, which had once been used as a satellite office.

Well we couldn't use that particular cable, but one night we arranged for a second smaller one to be strung across the road. I have no idea how my staff managed it, but the next day we were in business and we thrived.

I particularly liked the fact that my office in The Elephant House had a fire escape and whenever a particularly unpleasant client would arrive demanding to see me, my secretary would alert me and I would rush down the fire escape and take refuge in a small café up the road until the coast was clear!

Once the company became a subsidiary of News International the culture inevitably changed. We had a security review, which meant a fire alarm was fitted to my escape door. For a while I managed to disable it before I fled the building, but matters came to a head when the new security guard from HQ spotted me taking a short cut up the iron stairs back to my office and started chasing me up the stairs – completely unaware that I was the CEO.

These experiences made me very aware that every company has its own *Company Consciousness* – a symbiosis of its culture, geography, CEO, Board, shareholders and bankers. Each work together to produce the business, but the company itself will also have its own identity and influence on those with whom it engages. I call this influence a *Spiritual Footprint*, which manifests on both an individual and corporate level and also is a function of the industry in which the company operates.

Spiritual Footprints

For example, if you've ever been to a casino you'll have noticed a particular grasping energy. I call it greed – but whatever it is, it's not pure and it creates very profound damage to the psyche. The ancient Indian texts repeatedly warn against the harm caused by dice games and you would be well advised to stay clear of any industry that has gambling at its heart. Furthermore, a tobacco company, because of the deadly consequences of its product, will produce a negative influence, even if the people working within it are wonderful. At some level we FEEL what we're doing is bad for us, but we go ahead and do it anyway! And then we think we're so 'sophisticated'.

We DO appear unique in the animal kingdom in our ability to wake up at night and worry, to place ourselves in endless meetings, to work until we drop (even if our lives don't depend on it), and to eat a sandwich over a spreadsheet. We make products packed full of chemicals and fat, eat them and then wonder why cancer rates are increasing. We don't worry about the effects our companies are having, their Spiritual Footprint in the wider world.

I was watching the TV show 'Madmen' about the advertising industry in the sixties (which should be part of any curriculum on Enlightened Business as it accurately portrays how we began to lose track with reality and replace functionality with aspiration). Advertising now brainwashes us into buying products because they make us feel sexy, rather than doing anything useful.

Anyway, in the particular episode I was watching the main characters, Don and Betty, go for a picnic with their kids. When it's time to go Don throws a Coke can at some distant trees and Betty discards the used bags on the grass. As their car drives into the distance, the camera stays focused on the abandoned trash.

The audience is shocked by their disregard for the environment, because today we are more aware, more conscious of how we are related to our surroundings.

Business, however, has been slower in recognizing its connection to the wider world.

In business we recognize cycles. An executive who can tap into trends and future fashions, whether in clothes, food or technology, is highly prized. We have to extend our horizons, to raise our consciousness and see that there are actual trends in nature that we have to be aware of if we are to be fulfilled in our individual lives and in our companies.

Raising consciousness is what we seek to do all day long. We spend hours on the internet searching for information that will make us more knowledgeable. Knowledge is power. Higher consciousness is like looking at the world from an elevated vantage point. A truck may be heading round a bend at breakneck speed towards an oncoming car, but if its driver could see from the point of view of a helicopter he would be able to see the car heading towards him and slow down. Without that extra perception he might very well crash – and this is the situation we're in today.

We learn at school about the 'survival of the fittest', which means that there will always be some whom are not fit for purpose and will drop away. We normally think of this in terms of the adaptation of man and the species, but it is true at every level. Once we see this literally 'at work' then we can understand and accept why companies grow, then sometimes fade away; why fashions come and go; and why there is a constant interest in innovation and 'progress'.

So our company may thrive or fail, but in every case those involved will be learning much-needed lessons and nature will use the corporate asset in the best way it can. This is because nature does not have countless committees and think-tanks to work through and can just act spontaneously and impulsively.

Natural Cycles

Yes, there are bigger forces at play and nature gives us all the examples we need to get us back on track and to raise our individual and company consciousness. For instance, here is an excerpt from an article by Carl Zimmer that I found in a November 2007 edition of the *New York Times*:

Americans spend 3.7 billion hours a year in congested traffic. But you will never see ants stuck in gridlock.

Army ants, which Dr. Couzin has spent much time observing in Panama, are particularly good at moving in swarms. If they have to travel over a depression in the ground, they erect bridges so that they can proceed as quickly as possible.

'They build the bridges with their living bodies,' said Dr. Couzin, a mathematical biologist at Princeton University and the University of Oxford. 'They build them up if they're required, and they dissolve if they're not being used.'

A typical ant swarm can have over a million members all working perfectly in harmony. Is this insectoid communism, or hive-mind capitalism? Does it matter? Their whole community is focused on doing what must be done to maximise the survival of the community – not just the profits.

How do they do that? How is it possible? And how can we apply this perspective to our collective organisations – our companies – to maximise their potential?

As far as I am aware an ant is not self-conscious, nor would it spend hours developing strategy or hire management consultants to tell it what it knows already. But with the level of consciousness it does have it far outstrips all economic and social models the brightest human brains have thus far been able to dream up.

In the animal kingdom we notice the extraordinary way in which animals 'know' exactly what their 'job' is. We suspect that animals have no self-consciousness. We humans talk of the conscious mind which is deciding and the 'sub-conscious' mind, and then we make the massive assumption that our 'subconscious' plays no active part in our decision making process – AND that we are superior to animals. However, certain animals (whales, dolphins, monkeys, dogs and cats to name just a few) clearly demonstrate attributes of higher intelligence.

A wonderful friend of mine in Australia called Howie Cooke spends his time campaigning – at the moment about the whale trade – but his 'work' has taken him round the world on a variety of environmental issues. Howie has a symbiotic relationship with dolphins and will often take friends out to spend time with his dolphin pals, who in turn play practical jokes on their visitors such as hiding under the boat and playing 'boo'.

Of course, in our self-delusion we imagine that we alone amongst our animal neighbours have the ability to reason. But block an animal from doing what it has to do and it will work a way around the problem, which might include eating you!

Which leads to an interesting observation: IF an animal is not self-conscious, the reasoning must be taking place in its unconscious mind and must be synonymous with instinct.

It was remarkable how many animals went to higher ground just before the 2004 Tsunami struck parts of Asia. Likewise, a friend who was on holiday in Thailand at that time suddenly had an urge (instinct again) to move his family out of his hotel early one morning. He could not explain his feelings, but he was so agitated his family went along with him and they hurriedly packed up their belongings and headed off in their hired car. Shortly after they left the tsunami struck their hotel, destroying it and causing harm to those remaining.

To explain these phenomena, we could say that animals act according to their Group Consciousness and that any group, be it a family, nation or company will act depending on the level, integration, and purity of its overall consciousness.

The Body Corporate

Companies are the best-placed organisms on the global stage to facilitate rapid change. But their consciousness is inextricably entwined with the
'ciousness of their staff, their Board and their shareholders. So for
'nies to change, individuals must change first and this impetus has to
'h the CEO.

lese, a company is called a 'body corporate' in recognition of the
'iccessful company will act harmoniously as a single entity.

' call the CEO the brains behind the outfit. Their job is not only to steer the company forward but also to be plugged into trends both in the marketplace and in the wider world. He will set the ethos and culture for the whole business.

It's his job to get the big ideas and these probably occur – as they do with everyone – during moments of relaxation: listening to music, dropping off to sleep, out of nowhere at 3am, or in the shower under the warm flow of water. So perhaps it's the unconscious mind noodling away?

I would dare to suggest that perhaps he's tapping into the evolutionary flow and the collective unconscious for his inspiration. Then he needs to go back to his Board and executives and 'translate' his vision into a language they understand and in a way that can be comprehended at their different levels of consciousness. Everyone will interpret the message differently depending on their conditioning – but overall – if the CEO does a good job, they'll get the message.

However to communicate effectively the CEO will have to use that mysterious skill: charisma. If you Google 'charisma', one definition you'll get is: 'A special divine gift which endows the recipient with a supernatural ability to know and proclaim the will of God... (from the Greek).'

But how can the CEO be a spiritual leader? When I think of a spiritual leader, the Dalai Lama comes to mind. The Dalai Lama is far from being a businessman, but his 'job' is to be a spiritual leader and to make decisions, both spiritual and economic, which affects the lives of millions of   people who find his discourses elevating, no matter what walk of life they come from.

In his book *The Art of Happiness at Work*, the Dalai Lama says his job is doing 'nothing'. Of course he is extremely active, but the lesson is that anyone involved in business should be acting completely naturally from a deep inner resource and that this action should feel instinctive. The Dalai Lama also states in his book that the purpose of life is happiness and that this is determined more by your state of mind than by external conditions, circumstances and events.

As we've already discussed, a truly effective business leader would have an almost uncanny knack of being both decisive and also able to take on board the needs of both his company and its relationship to the marketplace.

Watch a successful business leader 'at work' and you will see that he or she makes decisions spontaneously and with little thought. Richard Branson, for example, travels the world with a small notepad in which he jots down each idea and then keeps them for future reference. He's also a bit of a techno-phobe, but despite that has a natural ability to spot new trends in any field. For him, solutions and ideas will 'appear' 'out of nowhere' (or so it seems) and he will run with them.

Recently I was reading an interview with Sir Martin Sorrell of WPP fame, who according to the article tells 'stressed' executives they should be having more fun. That sums it up for me, because the best ideas come when you're relaxed and enjoying yourself.

Often within a company, the tendency is to stick with the comfortable. In my own case, whenever I came up with another 'genius' idea my compatriots would try and talk me down, because on the surface they saw problems rather than solutions.

Being a successful CEO means having the consciousness to tap into the universal flow combined with the practicality and persistence to make things happen. You also need the humbleness to feel when things are going 'off-track' and to change accordingly.

I struggled for two years to set up my discounted telephony project, which became SkyTalk. I knew that the stranglehold the large telecom companies had on the industry would be eroded by new technology. I was certain that if I invested a considerable sum in setting up a new call centre, it would help me secure the business.

All my colleagues thought I was barking mad – but I persisted and I got the gig. In this particulat instance I just knew I was onto something, and it all came together.

Higher Purpose

Once the dynamics of business are seen as a co-venture with evolution, it is easier to see why many people become obsessed by their careers, because on the evolutionary level, companies provide an important tool.

It is essential that the CEO and Chairman (who, incidentally, is the 'soul' of any company), must both have a clear idea of where the company's strategy lies, where it sits in the world and what its overall consciousness and purpose are. By referring back to the company's objective in the world and then with reference to its day-to-day activities, a company is opening itself up to information from nature itself.

These days little emphasis or acknowledgement is given to the higher purpose of companies, so it is even more important that their vision is shared articulately with other Directors and that Directors are chosen not only for their experience, network and skill set, but for their own ability to understand and articulate that vision to their own departments to enhance the vision of the CEO. Just like the example of the ants, everyone in the company must be working together to achieve the common goal.

This works more easily in small companies and those where the founder is still active in the business. A Founder fired by tenacity, luck, intelligence and charm will always stand a good chance of defeating a faceless corporation. Rupert Murdoch is the driving force behind News Corp and he remains full of passion for the media business (particularly newspapers) and has oodles of charm. These factors, I suspect, contributed to his success in buying *The Wall Street Journal.*

Similarily, muuch has been much written about the impact of Starbucks on independent coffee shops and also the spread of the American culture worldwide. I do not feel comfortable pontificating and judging – if I can possibly help myself avoid it, that is. As a lover of both my local coffee shop and my local Starbucks, I would feel sad if either disappeared. And I also have to confess a warm glow when I see a Starbucks at a foreign airport and I can slip in for a furtive chai latte.

The point on leadership, however, is that Howard Schultz, the driver and leader behind Starbucks, appears to have had a spiritual vision for his company and that has lead to its phenomenal success. I hope that this can be sustained when he eventually steps down.

Conversely, where a company has been around for many decades or where a bank has bought it because it was interested mainly in returns, then keeping the company performing successfully becomes more challenging.

Most founders will tell you that money is not their key driver, but a by-product of their success. Yet, beneath the founders, managers tend to make profit the only benchmark, without recognising that it is the result of a balanced, healthy company.

You will have noticed how often a Founder sells a company to a conglomerate or private equity house, and then the company fails. The Founder then buys it back for a dollar, builds it back up again and then sells it once more a few years later – this happens all the time.

A company run *just* to make money will often fail. It might take a few years but without a clear vision coming from a charismatic CEO and supportive Board, trading will be that much harder.

Another cause for concern is when there is disharmony anywhere within the company. This shows disharmony within the body corporate. In a human this imbalance would be symbolised by a disease, which could be minor or terminal. We talk about companies being sick, or sleeping giants because we know intuitively that they have their own *company consciousness.*

So a successful company must be 'awake' and free from confrontation. Confrontations are about ego. When a sense of separation occurs so that an individual executive is thinking from the smaller ego-self instead of the company consciousness (and especially if it becomes about fear or power) then there is a disconnection and the company will to some degree become unstable.

For this reason, amongst many others, it is so important to ensure that Board constitution is correct and the existing Board must exercise rigorous examination of their gut feelings before appointing a new member. Particular problems can also arise when through a process of raising additional finance or takeover the Board suddenly has an influx of outside nominee Directors.

For the past few years I have been working as a Non-Executive Director, sometimes as a Nominee of a venture capital (VC) concern, and often in start-up situations. Sometimes I feel that I have been invaluable in being able to facilitate communication between management and the VC. However there have been occasions when there have been very wide disparities between the investor and the investee – too wide for me to bridge, and I have felt more comfortable extricating myself. There needs to be an alignment or at least a sympathetic match between the consciousnesses of both sides.

Private Equity Groups have, of course, got their own unique consciousness and these will differ from one to another. But one of the key considerations is to what extent they are focused on making a sizeable short-term return as opposed to the degree to which they are supportive and understanding of management's needs for long-term capital and a mutual realistic assessment of the time before there is a positive cashflow.

This discussion naturally leads us to consider the shareholder base.

Enlightened Shareholders

Whenever I'm asked to become involved in a new project, particularly at Board level, I carefully analyse the shareholder register to see if there are likely be conflicts with my way of doing business.

With shareholders I check and see how they made their own money and whether they have been in any legal disputes, and I assess whether they are people who will help or hinder the project should there be any difficult trading issues. I like to know where else they have invested their funds and how these investments worked out.

Every company or individual brings influence related to their past actions to your project. It's no surprise that a successful investment fund is good to associate with, whereas a shareholder who has been embroiled in countless legal disputes will heighten the risk of YOU spending months in court!

Most businesspeople know intuitively that corporate history tends to repeat itself, yet it is surprising how many folks I know do this necessary due diligence after the investment – when it is too late to change horses. Once you understand that corporations have their own consciousness and Spiritual Footprint, you can see why this due diligence is fundamentally important.

This then is a question of short-termism. Are the investors purely interested in a return – and after how long, three years or three months? It is increasingly difficult to find shareholders who are prepared to be patient with a business and its management.

Short-cuts in the intuitive due diligence process are often taken when the company is in a hurry to raise funds.

Many companies need to raise outside finance at some point, to fuel growth, cash-flow or for acquisition. But when you bring in an outsider you also align yourself with their destiny! The situation can become even more confused when it comes to raising loans.

The simplest approach is to issue new equity in return for straightforward investment, because taking loans cedes control away from the company towards bankers whose only interest is in a financial return. It also drains the company of its full potential because money goes into interest payments rather than growing the business.

If the business secures a loan, then it is important that the interest level should be set low in order to enhance the prospect of growth rather than ensuring that the company treads water because it is trading simply to pay interest. For management, the other side of the coin is to treat investors as supportive family members. You have to feel free to be truthful and open and to trust them to be supportive in times of growth or, alternatively, trouble.

It is my opinion that international encouragement of widespread share ownership has done business a disservice. Individuals are being encouraged to invest in areas in which they have little or no expertise or interest. There is little difference to me in investing in a small publicly quoted company than going to the races – except if you invested a considerable proportion of your life savings on a racehorse you might realise how reckless this was. And yet people spend and lose considerable sums on the advice of their broker in areas that are completely outside their knowledge zone.

Enlightened Business demands complete alignment between the aspirations of management and shareholders. Sadly, the rising trend in short-termism will lead to increasing tensions and we are already witnessing the consequences. Fear-based investors lurch from market to market, from shares to commodities, from currency to currency, purely concerned with keeping and increasing what they have. Their attachment and fear, rather than trust, has an opposite effect in effective trading, as we see around us every day.

The solution is to take a more traditional approach and to move business back to its roots of simple trading. So let us look at a couple of companies and see if we can assess their company consciousness.

Assessing Company Consciousness
What is the consciousness of many banking firms? Look at the recent example of Lehman Brothers, which just days before it filed for bankruptcy transferred $8 billion from its UK arm in Europe back to its New York HQ to prop up its core U.S. business. This meant, of course, that its UK staff might not be paid whilst its American counterparts could receive significant bonuses.

Hedge funds in particular get a bad press. Why is this? It's because they combine gambling with negative energy. By shorting stock, irrespective of the underlying performance of a company, consciousness is focused on failure – which subtly affects the fortunes of the shorted company. This is the reason why there is an intuitive dislike of these funds. The banking industry is there to support business, so that people can earn a 'honest' crust. The short burst a trader gets by make a 'killing' is at a cost to those who may lose their jobs as a result – which always involves a negative tradeoff.

By comparison let's look at Triodos Bank:

Triodos bank was established in the Netherlands in 1980 by an economist, a professor in tax law, a senior organisational consultant and a banker. It only lends to organisations who create social, environmental or cultural value and it has backed wind and solar power initiatives, organic farming and regional regeneration projects.

It's a public company, with around 3000 shareholders and 2.4 billion euros of funds under management. However, unlike The Body Shop, there is coherence between the shareholder base, Board and employees. The issue for the Body Shop was always the tension between the campaigning and the fact that The Body Shop was a skincare and cosmetics company. Anyone investing in The Body Shop in its early days would have been unclear if they were putting money into an anti-war campaign or developing a nut oil.

There is no such confusion with Triodos bank, who are clear and transparent about their aims and these are supported by their investor base. I admire Triodos because it is one of the few businesses that seem to be acting holistically at every level. They involve their staff in the development of the business and their investee companies speak highly of their input. Also, although it is almost impossible to be certain about the outcome of any action, it is hard to envisage a Triodos investment doing anything but good.

I'm sure anyone connected with Triodos would feel comfortable talking about the activities of the bank – even in the middle of the current recession.

Moving back to the tobacco example, here's a quote from the World Health Organisation (WHO) website:

'Tobacco is the second major cause of death in the world. It is currently responsible for the death of one in ten adults worldwide (about 5 million deaths each year). If current smoking patterns continue, it will cause some 10 million deaths each year by 2020. Half the people that smoke today – that is about 650 million people – will eventually be killed by tobacco.' (source: www.who.int/tobacco/health_priority/en/index.html)

A tobacco company may have begun life long before tobacco was a known health hazard, as an altruistic enterprise giving a livelihood to local farmers and labourers and providing a product to be consumed for relaxation. But now the overriding consciousness of the company, its *raison d'etre*, must be to spread disease.

Let me explain: The company itself will have its share of heroes of villains. Staff benefits may be excellent, shareholders may be enjoying excellent returns and customers may be delighted with the quality of the tobacco, BUT in karmic terms, at some level everyone associated with the venture is responsible for its consequences.

As I constantly stress, we need to wake up. The tobacco industry cannot be spiritually enhancing, although it can still be full of wonderful people. People like you and me who may feel a little uneasy about what they are doing, but push their doubts to the back of their minds where they niggle away. The same can be true of any industry if the intent isn't right. To widen our perspective let's look briefly at the broader example of the drug industry. You might think that working in a drug company, which exists to find cures for people's ailments would be a wonderful opportunity. But then, as I read in the *New York Times*, November 2004:

'*A detailed reconstruction of Merck's handling of Vioxx, based on interviews and internal company documents, suggests that actions the company took – and did not take – soon after the drug's safety was questioned may have affected the health of potentially thousands of patients, as well as the company's financial health and reputation.*'

Here again the positive aims associated with the health care industry were compromised for the sake of profits. All of which suggests that even the most altruistic company or industry can be thwarted in its aims by short-termism and a singular focus on money.

As mentioned before, an industry that is well known to create a negative influence in the world in pursuit of profit is modern advertising. Advertising encourages us to consume and 'live the dream'. But we are in the dream right now. We are bombarded by messages that reinforce the idea that we need a new car, dress, or house, etc. Advertising says there is something wrong with us if we don't have the latest phone or whichever product they are being paid to advertise.

The real danger is that is doesn't just end there. The Madison Avenue advertising industry has exported this illusion around the world in search of bigger profits, and in doing so is adversely affecting foreign culture and individual identities. Unilever, for example, is looking to export deodorants to Asia. As quoted in the May 26, 2008 *London Times*:

'*[They are] dreaming up advertisements that will induce shame about sweat stains across the region...*'

As the global vice-president for Axe, the division that makes deodorant (which is marketed as Lynx in Britain) says in the same article:

'Asia is a market we have never really cracked. They don't think they smell, but people everywhere smell.'

To him and his advertising mindset, Asia is 'the last empty space on the map' for global deodorants, worth billions of pounds.

Interestingly, this statement is absolutely true. People everywhere smell, but any one who travels frequently in Asia will tell you that even the most humble Indian villager will be spotlessly clean, as cultural cleanliness is inculcated from an early age and they bathe frequently (sometimes twice a day). And Indians also have excellent teeth because they use natural 'toothpastes' and don't (yet) exist on a diet of doughnuts, hamburgers and sweets.

Advertising is NOT inherently 'bad'. It's dishonesty that creates a bad feeling.

So you see, whether the company is dealing with an end product or service in any field – like food, tobacco, banking, advertising or medicine, to use the quoted examples, the nature of the company's consciousness will still alter and affect its consumers, employees and suppliers. And no company is immune to this. If we are to remain true to ourselves we have to ensure that all products and services we produce are honest, do not produce a sense of lack or inferiority in our customers and do not seek to undermine the cultures in which we are trading.

I have given some straightforward examples above, but normally situations are more complicated.

When I owned my company, I turned down any business from the tobacco giants, but when I sold to News International I felt obliged to soften this approach and merely *discouraged* any tobacco accounts. I was troubled by my own softness and now regret that I did not enforce my no-tobacco rule, even after the takeover. I used intellect to justify my weakness. The new owners won't understand, I thought. How can one part of the Group have tobacco clients and another refuse them?

But the decision to soften my approach was entirely mine, and was part of a process of compromise that eventually led to my own demise. Because loss of direction comes in small stages. It's rarely the case that happiness in a job suddenly turns sour and that is why we must always be vigilant.

As we discussed earlier, it is fundamentally important that before you begin any business enterprise or take a new job you examine on an emotional level whether it 'feels' right for you.

But as your company becomes more mainstream it's harder to know in a clear-cut way what purpose the company serves from the perspective of the greater good. Many people would assume that an arms company would also be in the 'bad guys' category – but others would argue that such a company was 'defending the free world'. It's easy to consign the gambling industry to the 'bad' box, but is bingo really so awful? And terrible things are said about the drinks industry, but a glass of wine may prevent a heart attack. It's all a question of scale…

However you will get a clear feeling, literally, on the company you keep – or more precisely, the company that keeps you. If you work for a tobacco company ask yourself how you'd feel about your children smoking. And if you work for a juice company, how does the idea of your children drinking fresh organic juice appeal? I am sure you prefer the juice example!

Assessing your company's consciousness is simply a matter of putting yourself in the shoes of your customers and suppliers, thinking of them as family members and then assessing yourself how they might feel about your company's products and its corporate culture.

People working within companies may be inherently good, and might have the best of intentions, but their conditioning, weaknesses, peer pressure and focus on profit compromise them by small degrees. We are free to make choices which are not life-supporting, but we must realise there is always a consequence to every action.

But if we can wake up to the connection of our actions and their wider consequences, we would transform not just ourselves and the companies we work in, but our world – and that is my challenge to you.

The rise in consciousness that we are all part of is breaking through self-limiting beliefs and making us appreciate that, in fact, we are far more powerful than we realise – so that if we were to speak our feelings we might be pleasantly surprised by the level of support we would receive.

You are not alone in recognising there has to be a different way, but if you do not speak your truth you will not find that out and the harsh corporate culture will endure longer. But if you tune into your destiny then the universe will also give you all the tools you need to change your world – and the bravery to act.

You simply have to take the first step according to what level you are in your organisation. And regardless of where that is, you are in a more powerful position than you realise.

And you have free will, so be conscious of what's going on, speak out and change whatever is in your field of influence and if you're still uncomfortable then get another job if you possibly can. Your life is too important to spend your time doing anything other than being yourself and having fun so don't compromise for less.

I began this chapter talking about Broadsystem and I'll end it in Skipton, an old Yorkshire Town, because this is where Broadsystem's current owners are based. Broadsystem was sold by News International to Skipton Information Group, which is part of the Skipton Building Society, which was established in 1853.

I suspect nobody in Skipton is aware that Broadsystem once traded out of a recording studio. It has now become part of the establishment, run from a market town in the North of England. My informal, rule-free, rather anarchic baby has joined a pillar of British Tradition and orthodoxy.

Who'd have guessed?

WORKBOOK:

Companies, like individuals, have their own sense of consciousness. Make a list of your favourite companies and explain why you like them, what it is that distinguishes them from other competitors.

_____

_____

_____

_____

_____

_____

_____

_____

The purpose of a company described in its mission statement may change along with evolution. What's your company's mission statement, and has it changed or drifted in practice from what it claims to be?

_____

_____

_____

_____

_____

_____

_____

_____

A conscious company must be flexible and facilitate empowerment of the individuals which form it. Responsibility is necessary at every level: the Board, staff, suppliers and customers. Can you see this applying to your business, and if not, why not? How could your company empower all its staff?

_____

_____

_____

_____

_____

_____

_____

A good business leader will be charismatic, mercurial and have a vibrant connection to his own purpose and that of his company. List some of your favourite business leaders both here and abroad and compare the qualities that you like about them.

The shareholders themselves have a responsibility to invest in companies they believe in. If you own shares can you claim this is true for you? List why or why not. Conversely, look at your company's shareholder base and see if it is aligned with your company's objectives.

Each company has its own greater purpose, which may or may not, according to your own beliefs, align with you. Can you state your company's purpose (this may be different to its mission statement). Does it align with your beliefs – and if not why are you still working there?

Chapter 7

An Evolving Business Model

Those who use constructive imagination to see how much they can give for
a dollar instead of how little they can give for a dollar, are bound to succeed.

Henry Ford

Whether you look at the financial, environmental or social headlines of late you would probably agree that the world is in a dire state of affairs and something must be done to rectify matters.

A just and sustainable world is what is needed and because companies are so powerful and can produce far-reaching changes across our planet, it is likely that companies and the business cycle which drives them will play a core part in this transformation.

The business model we currently trade under, however, is not the beginning nor the end of the line. The world's first multi-nationals were the British East India Company (established in 1600) and the Dutch East India Company (1602). In those days, as you can see by their names, national political and trading interests were combined such that the corporation was effectively an agent of the state.

So you can see that the global financial system has evolved over centuries to its current apex, where multinationals (perhaps you work for one!) now have a power previously reserved for, and possibly exceeding those of governments.

A 1999 report by the MIT historian Bruce Mazlish, quoting from UN statistics, declared that of the 100 largest economic entities in the world, 51 were multinational corporations and these were wealthier than over 120 nation-states (see www.gatt.org/trastat_e.html).

And that was before the boom time for transnational corporations during the first half of the current decade. Now sales figures are not exactly comparable with GDP and there are a lot of other variables and ways to measure wealth. But one thing is certain – the balance of power has shifted, and even in these currently volatile economic times companies are as, or more powerful, than many countries.

The end result of this profit-based capitalism by country or corporation is a massive gap between rich and poor. A 2006 report titled The World Distribution of Household Wealth by the World Institute for Development Economics Research of the United Nations University (www.wider.unu.edu)

declared that 10% of adults accounted for 85% of global household wealth, whilst the number of people living on less than $1 a day was over a billion – a number that is increasing.

If we feel this is nothing to do with us we are misguided. Firstly, growing poverty and polarisation of wealth leads to increasing crime and terrorism. Secondly, poverty is collateral damage from our capitalist system, which focuses only on profit and ensures that the rich get richer.

We are all involved and we only have to look around us to see the consequences of our current ignorance. We are destroying our natural habitat, food and fuel prices are rising and the economy lurches from crisis to crisis. This is happening because we are ignoring our inner voices and standing against our destiny.

But if we do not listen and continue in the same manner as the past, then we will arrive at our destiny through suffering.

In short, we have to become enlightened business people who adopt a holistic approach to our lives. We have to work on ourselves to raise our own state of consciousness and then to also work within our own companies to expand the range of thinking and responsibility. And we have to do it NOW!

Bill Gates and many other business leaders have woken up to the holistic model and are doing their fair share to redress the balance. Gates is now devoting his time to distributing his wealth through the Bill and Melinda Gates Foundation in an attempt to eradicate diseases like malaria. He is single-handedly doing more than some governments in the area of health research.

This is awesome but the fact remains that if we perpetuate the existing business of cold capitalism it will only lead to a growing number of poor people as the accumulated wealth is distributed unevenly.

To quote from Jeffrey Frieden's book *Global Capitalism*, referring to China:

'By 2000 the average urban household had three times the income of the average rural household, a much greater multiple than in 1985. Shanghai was one of the world's great industrial and commercial centers, with more than half of the Fortune 500 companies present, but there are still nearly two hundred million Chinese living in poverty.'

This situation is mirrored across the 'developing' world, particularly in Africa. So merely bringing people into the capitalist system does not mean that a society will uniformly benefit. And the term 'better off' is a relative term. Are people better off if they live in an isolated and hostile city, living in squalor or sleeping in drainpipes (as you'll witness in India) and sending money 'back home' to their village? Is this quality of life and is it truly 'better off'?

An Evolving Business Model

The ice-cream company Ben & Jerry's summarise this well on their website:

'Capitalism and the wealth it produces do not create opportunity for everyone equally. We recognise that the gap between the rich and the poor is wider than at anytime since the 1920's. We strive to create economic opportunities for those who have been denied them and to advance new models of economic justice that are sustainable and replicable. By definition, the manufacturing of products creates waste. We strive to minimise our negative impact on the environment.'

The almost universal acceptance of capitalism as the international monetary system of choice has led to the corporate belief that business is solely about the generation of profit. This belief is embedded so strongly in our culture that the idea that there should be other objectives might seem näive. Of course, the basic welfare of workers is essential if the profit potential is to be maximised, and recently there has been a shift towards some degree of corporate social responsibility. But the central focus is always on profit.

The capitalist model seems to honour many of the values that make us human: We want a decent and improving standard of living, we want to express ourselves and we want to do something we are passionate about – but this focus on profit has led to greed, envy, excess and imbalance. It also has led to the instability and inequalities we are witnessing today, and calls by members of the global economic community – led by voices like British Prime Minister Gordon Brown and the French President Nicolas Sarkozy – for a new mode of capitalism; different from the current profit-led one.

As Brown said in his seminal article in the Washington Post on Oct 17, 2008:

'The global problems we face require global solutions. At the end of World War II, American and European visionaries built a new international economic order and formed the International Monetary Fund, the World Bank and a world trade body. They acted because they knew that peace and prosperity were indivisible. They knew that for prosperity to be sustained, it had to be shared. Such was the impact of what they did for their day and age that Secretary of State Dean Acheson spoke of being "present at the creation."

Today, the same sort of visionary internationalism is needed to resolve the crises and challenges of a different age. And the greatest of global challenges demands of us the boldest of global cooperation.

The old postwar international financial institutions are out of date. They have to be rebuilt for a wholly new era in which there is global, not national, competition and open, not closed, economies. International flows of capital are so big they can overwhelm individual governments. And trust, the most precious asset of all, has been eroded ...

Confidence about the future is vital to building confidence for today. We must deal with more than the symptoms of the current crisis. We have to tackle the root causes. So the next stage is to rebuild our fractured international financial system.'

Like it or lump it, a total transformation of the current capitalist system is on its way. But to avoid the mistakes of the past we must be honest in appraising not just the mistakes and weaknesses of our current system, but in analysing why they manifested.

How Did We Get Here?

We've mentioned the current capitalist obsession with profit as a major flaw in a sustainable global paradigm. But where did that profit drive originate from? The oft-called 'father of modern economics', Scottish philosopher Adam Smith (1723-1790), was responsible for the idea that rational self-interest was at the heart of all economic transactions and that an 'invisible hand' guided free markets, two central tenets that have led to the cultural drift towards our current profit obsession.

In his magnum opus – *An Inquiry into the Nature and Causes of the Wealth of Nations,* written in 1776, Smith also promoted another basic flaw at the heart of capitalism – the 'Division of Labour' – which affects us all and is still embraced to this day.

Smith advocated that tasks should be broken down into tiny parts and given to workers whose only job is to specialise. Prior to the Industrial Revolution, a craftsman would be responsible for the entire production of his 'product', but Smith demonstrated that this was inefficient and that productivity would be improved if each element of the task was separated and given to different components of the work force.

Much of 'modern' labour practices have evolved from his ideas, including assembly lines and the establishment of unions to protect Labour. Traditional capitalism encourages employees to be treated as 'human assets' and it enshrines the idea that profit through increased productivity is at the heart of business.

Now Smith wasn't a bad chap. He realised that assembly-line work would become stultifying and boring and proposed 'worker education' as the antidote. Since Smith wrote his masterpiece we've had over 200 years to formulate modifications to his original capitalist blueprint. But because we have not radically evolved our thinking about capitalism, we still tend to think about our enterprises in ways that do not honour us, or our business partners – be they employees, shareholders or suppliers. And things have been this way for a long time.

Consider this quote by the well-known economist John Maynard Keynes, referring to a period just before the outbreak of World War I in 1914:

'The inhabitant of London could order by telephone, sipping his morning tea in bed, the various products of the whole earth, in such quantity as he might see fit, and reasonably expect their early delivery upon his doorstep... he could secure forthwith, if he wished it, cheap and comfortable means to any country or climate without passport or other formality... and could proceed abroad to foreign quarters, without knowledge of their religion, language, or customs, bearing coined wealth upon his person, and would consider himself greatly aggrieved and much surprised at the least interference.'

Keynes was referring to the lot of the average businessperson in the *early* years of the 20th century. Then there was very little to stop the international trader conducting his affairs anywhere he desired either in person (without a passport!) or by sending a representative.

Jeffrey A Frieden, in his recent book *Global Capitalism,* quotes Keynes and then explains that in the early 20th century there was an international movement towards free trade and an adoption by many countries of the 'gold standard', whereby a currency could be converted into gold at a pre-set exchange rate. The consequent ease of currency conversion with the certain backing of gold greatly facilitated global trade.

The United States, the United Kingdom, most of Europe and Scandinavia had adopted the gold standard before the Great War and coupled with the telephone and telegraph, market information was available within seconds. We could, at this point, wonder how anybody could devise a financial system based on linking the value of a currency to that of a lump of metal (gold) – but as already discussed, the whole edifice of our economic system crumbles if we focus too much on the detail – so we'll move on.

Since 1914, there has been a century of instability characterised by enormous suffering, punctuated by periods of relative calm. World War I was followed by the Great Depression in 1929 and throughout the 1930s. Banks crashed, inflation (particularly in Germany) was catastrophic, unemployment and food shortages were common, World War II almost led to the destruction of the free world as we know it and since then, although peace broke out in Europe, millions of people live in fear of starvation or violence, throughout Africa and elsewhere in the world.

Throughout the post-war period, governments and their advisors attempted to predict market trends in order to produce financial stability. But this is predicated on the assumption that prices are predictable in the first place, which of course they are not.

Capitalism itself has also been a lot more volatile than the bastions of industry might have you believe. Just look at the current US $2 trillion plus bailout of the American banking system and the cries of socialist intervention!

But governments have invoked free trade and protectionism; they have adopted the gold standard and abandoned it. They have advocated total government intervention and no government intervention at all. Before the Great Depression it was fashionable to advocate no government manipulation of the economy. An economy in decline was treated like an invalid. It was considered natural to 'purge' society of the evils of high prices and wages. After the 'necessary' suffering caused by unemployment and hyper-inflation it was thought that the economy would self-correct.

This seemed to be the case in the early years of the 20th century, just like the 21st, as governments were shocked into intervention to 'correct' their respective credit crises.

And while capitalism has been shifting gears, other 'isms' have also been fighting for their place in the sun. Although capitalism has been the overriding international economic system, communism appeared to offer a viable alternative midway through the 20th century and indeed, around 1960, it was being adopted throughout the Eastern Bloc. Ironically though, as communism began to disintegrate in the USSR in the late 1980s, the State colluded with entrepreneurs so that a small number of privileged oligarchs were handed national assets, making them some of the wealthiest individuals in the world.

Communism requires central planning and State-centralised control, and with that come all sorts of issues, from corruption and self-centredness to the thirst for power. Ironically, where communism is supposed to be about the power of the people, the historical example has tended to show that power is co-opted by small minorities for self-aggrandisement, and in that way it has been no different from capitalism

Are other models workable?

A social-based economic model was tried in Israel after its establishment in 1948 with the kibbutz system. The kibbutz community was intended to take care of its citizens from cradle to grave. It sounds good in theory: income is shared across the community and all inhabitants enjoy the same living conditions.

But in practice, unless true solidarity was maintained by individuals, resentment would arise and the power dynamic was still controlled by the Kibbutz Ruling Committee. It was the Committee who decided on innovations such as air-conditioning or kitchen installation, and thus regulated individual's natural urge to self-govern.

Recently I visited Meyer, a distant relative-by-marriage, who had emigrated to Israel from South Africa and spent most of his life there in a desire to live the Socialist Dream. His wife rather sheepishly cooked us a meal in her newly installed, but frugal kitchen. Previously, kibbutz members had to eat together in the central canteen and nobody cooked at home. Although the kibbutz canteen still functioned, each housing unit – by popular demand – had been granted a kitchen.

Of course such decisions affect every household and produce an enormous strain on central resources, as well as dispersing group energies. In this concrete example, I could see that the admirable aspirations and the ideals of the kibbutz, which dictated that every individual had to have the same living conditions, were gradually destroying the kibbutz itself.

This self-destructive tendency is at the heart of our economic system and our alienation from the land. It was first discussed by the ecologist Garrett Hardin in a seminal article entitled *Tragedy of the Commons,* in the journal *Science* in 1968.

Hardin used the theoretical example of herders sharing a common parcel of land (the 'Commons') on which they are all entitled to graze their cows. Each herder puts as many cows as possible onto the land even if the commons is damaged as a result. But if all herders make this individually rational decision, the commons is destroyed and all herders suffer.

The commons can be seen not just as land, but as the shared resource of all Earth's bounty, from the land and the sea, to advertising-free spaces and a pollution-free environment. Early on, before capitalism was even coined as a term, humans were cast into a survivalist mentality and forced to compete against one another for the resources of the Earth that we all need for our continued existence.

But that survival only happened on a large inter-tribal scale: in the immediate village or community people were taught that co-operation and sharing were paramount to the tribe's survival. And it is this instinctive knowledge of the shared ownership of Earth's commons that surfaced in the 20th century as communism, and in other social modalities like the kibbutz Meyer inhabits.

I wandered glumly through Meyers' kibbutz surveying the obvious poverty. Although nobody was starving, it was clear from the derelict and half-finished buildings and terrible food that this was an economic experiment gone badly wrong. Everyone I spoke to wanted to leave – but couldn't afford to. And yet despite that, the social idealism lived on.

Not every kibbutz in Israel is poor. Those kibbutzim that tinkered with the basic formulae to allow a measure of capitalist drive in the socialist template are relatively thriving. These kibbutzim realised that their inhabitants should be free to gain income outside the kibbutz and keep most of it (paying a central tax). Through this energetic / money stream they have built themselves better housing and they have embraced new technology, as well as new farming techniques.

And curiously, although the kibbutz movement has largely moved away from its idealistic principles, it is enjoying something of a renaissance, as yuppies from nearby towns are realising that their newfound wealth is not bringing fulfilment and they are coming back to kibbutzim in order to live in a more inclusive and sharing community. They are finding that a balance of both worlds – community and individualism – works best for them.

But back in the old style kibbutz Meyer, despite being in his 70s, still works for a meagre income and spends his spare time helping (even-more) underprivileged folk in the neighbouring Arab township. Any dream he had that his kibbutz would care for him in his old age has long disappeared.

And although he never regrets emigrating to Israel, he feels that he could have done more good outside of his kibbutz. Note, by the way, that Meyer never thinks of personal gain. His entire motivation is about what he can do to improve the lot of those around him. His disappointment is not that he has failed to accumulate sufficient capital for his retirement, but that he has not done enough for humanity.

So what lessons can we learn from all this? The lessons of Hardin's *Tragedy of the Commons* can be applied to any system. Capitalism needs to be modified to include a degree of socialism and a communist culture would need to be able to incorporate individual skills and desires. This is because each of us is different: we all have different skills and passions, but all of us are equal.

As money is really an energy that we channel around the planet, the mode of channelling that energy has been mutating to best fit the needs of the people on the ground. The consciousness directing the abundance of nature doesn't care if we humans accept its energy through the portal of capitalism, communism or socialism, as long as the energy is shared round effectively to keep the system running.

And like the progressive kibbutzim that have married the twin streams of communal living and support with a capital-driven incentive, the world now desperately needs a new paradigm to define how best to support ourselves.

But how do we devise that new paradigm, and can it be linked to economics alone?

Economobollocks

Economics is always looking for the 'Ultimate Theory' that will take the unpredictability out of the unpredictable.

Economic theories attempt to predict market trends to help governments' plan for the welfare of humankind. This would be all very well if human behaviour were predictable, and as entrepreneurs we are always trying to predict market trends ourselves. But most of us use gut instinct and some form of attunement to navigate our way in business.

Nassim Taleb in his book *Black Swan*, writes that nothing is that predictable because there will always be an unexpected event (the Black Swan). And once the unexpected happens, everyone rushes around trying to stop a recurrence. The attacks of 9/11 made airline travel more ghastly, but it did nothing to make terrorism less likely – in fact, it had perhaps the opposite effect.

Paul Ormerod, in his book *Butterfly Economics*, attempts to make a 'better' economic model based on the behaviour of ants, which because of the social nature of insect co-operation strategies, are used extensively to predict human behaviour. Ormerod mentions the example of an ant colony, which is presented with two food sources. Each source is constantly replenished. One would expect that once the first ant messenger randomly discovers one source, all the ants would flock to it. But in fact the ants favour one source and then the other in a seemingly random pattern, in a way that mirrors human economic market conditions!

Ormerod then demonstrates his new model, which seems to be more 'accurate' when looking at past events with the benefit of hindsight. It's hard to say if Ormerod's ant model or any other model theory would work in the unpredictable reality of the real world. But in the fantasy of the Narrative Story we project onto the world, we feel more comfortable when we believe we are in control of our destinies, so we have a deep in-built *need* for a theory, even if the reality is (currently) beyond our grasp.

Although various economic theories may be able to predict events for short periods, none have been proven to work over decades and when models fail, they do so in a spectacular fashion – as we are witnessing globally at the moment. The only thing that ultimately works in the changing template of global culture is our intuition, and as business people we need to nurture that.

So what is missing from the capitalist model and how can the existing system be modified?

Minimise Borrowing and Lending

The economist, activist and best-selling author John Perkins, in his book *Confessions of an Economic Hit Man,* paints a chilling picture of how he worked in collaboration with the United States government in large infrastructure projects in developing countries, justifying large loans from institutions such as the World Bank to finance them. These loans ensured that the 'target' countries would be forever beholden to the States and would need to return political and economic 'favours' in return.

I am sure that this is the way some of the world works, but Perkins demonstrates that at every level this way of doing business simply sheds unhappiness both in the local communities and amongst the executives who promulgate these policies.

Virtually every religion discourages the payment of interest on loans. As we discussed earlier, money is a form of energy that needs to be used to create. It is very admirable to help someone set up a business by granting a loan, providing the business is then not hampered for years with debt repayments.

We see the debt problem at every level of society and it is one of the major causes of tension in our world. As I write, many major financial institutions are in crisis because they are sitting on debts that they have granted but will not be repaid. They have encouraged homeowners to take out loans they cannot repay as the economy heads for a downwards spiral.

We are in the current credit crunch because we have taken on too much debt! This didn't happen overnight. When I grew up, debt was heavily discouraged. In fact, I remember when credit cards were first introduced as a status symbol and soon everyone wanted one. Debt is one of the greatest spiritual sicknesses because it produces an imbalanced energetic flow. It enslaves, breeds envy and encourages a grasping nature.

One of the greatest disservices governments do is to saddle students with debt and this becomes a habit that perpetuates through the banking system. In the West, people feel that debt is an entitlement to procure goods they can't afford. In Africa, credit cards are advertised as though they magically produced free money. And Western governments enslave weaker nations by funding projects and dictating policies or favours, whether in trade or defence.

I have been persuaded microfinance is good because when pure it encourages villagers in developing countries to become self-sufficient and start local enterprises. But too often the term is abused by loan sharks dressed in sheeps' clothing – to mix metaphors.

In the West though, banks have become ever less stringent in their criteria for granting loans, whilst consumer aspirations have become unrealistic. We are talking about the perception that everyone has to own their own home, have a car, air-conditioning, three holidays a year. Enough is never enough. There is always a bigger house and car, a better neighbourhood. And there is peer pressure and the need to impress and pretend you are someone else. Someone with more money or status.

When all of this is happening and everyone believes this is acceptable – then it is only a matter of time before someone realizes that the debt cannot ever be paid, EVER. And at that moment the bubble breaks and there is a realisation that – surprise surprise – the loans cannot be repaid – and there are an awful lot of loans.

And that is where the global economy finds itself right now – financially and spiritually bankrupt. The nationalisation of our financial institutions and the consequent resurgence of socialism has given an unparalleled opportunity to create a better, debt-free society – but this is not happening and the opportunity is being squandered.

Instead of encouraging prudence and compassion, governments are determined to restart the old system that brought us here in the first place!

Most of us realise that fulfillment and happiness do not come from accumulating money and assets. We know that sharing and empowering are more satisfying than greed and envy – it's just that we have been locked into fear for so long that we have forgotten the basic principles of life.

In this chapter we've looked at the capitalist system and its alternatives and seen that *any system can be used by evolution as long as it supports the needs and energies of the people it serves.*

As we progress through the first decade of the 21st century it is now obvious that the capitalist model, while still the most prevalent economic paradigm in modern society, needs to continue to evolve. We need to modify some of the basic concepts that we have been brainwashed into accepting so that our businesses can become spiritual lighthouses.

I had hoped that governments would lead the way through example and education into a new system – but this is not happening. Instead we must use the example of Bill Gates and consider how we can use the wealth generated by our companies to do some good in the world or even better, change our companies so that the wealth is distributed as it is generated back into society as whole and with the consent of shareholders.

The reward will be felt in the culture of our companies and the feeling of fulfillment that comes from helping those around us.

WORKBOOK:

Business is part of the eco-system in which we live. If all the participants (founders, shareholders and employees) only focus on profit they risk pulling themselves and those around them into a downwards spiral. Can you list some examples where your business dealings have not been solely about profit? Be truthful!

Any business must take into account the 'cost' of its practices on family life, welfare of its staff and impact on the community: a 'whole-systems theory' approach to business. List some of the fallout from your own business life on your personal, or your staff's personal lives.

Multinationals must consider the results of their trading on local cultures and have a responsibility to ensure these are respected and profits ploughed back into the communities that generate them. List some of your own examples of this, or of companies that you respect that give back to their communities.

Multinationals must be more prepared to collaborate rather than 'wage war' for the ultimate benefit of the human family which they serve. Can you think of some ways that multinational companies could practise this synergy? What are some examples from your own experience of collaboration?

_____

_____

_____

_____

_____

_____

_____

_____

Chapter 8

The New Global Age

Allegiance to growth is the most dominant feature of an economic and political system that has led us to the brink of disaster. Not to stand back now and question what has happened would be to compound failure with failure: failure of vision with failure of responsibility. Figuring out how to deliver prosperity without growth is more essential now than ever.

Tim Jackson, Sustainable Development Commission, 30th March 2009

Towards the end of 2008 I was trying to access my online savings account with the Icesave Bank when a message appeared: The website was experiencing 'technical difficulties'. I turned on the radio to hear that Icesave, a British subsidiary of Landsbanki, was in financial trouble, putting a new spin on the term 'technical'.

I had a substantial sum deposited in the bank. Losing that money wouldn't wipe me out, but it would certainly make a huge dent in my life savings and I realised the implications first-hand of the global connections that bind us all together in the world today. The value systems we had 'bought into' in the past decades were now coming back to haunt us and in this case Iceland itself appeared to be heading towards insolvency.

If my money had been in a UK bank account I might have had a better chance of recovering something – but Iceland?! The funny thing is that I knew the Icelandic economy was on the ropes, but I tied up my money in a six-month bond, which was due to mature the next week. I was praying that the bank would survive that long – but it didn't.

Like millions of people across the world I was hit by my own personal wave of economic turbulence from the global credit crisis. But as well as being a businessman I am also a meditation teacher and a spiritual person at heart. As I have argued throughout this book, I believe that a holistic approach to trading in the interdependent global marketplace is not just good practice – it's essential business. All very well in theory – but this was an interesting test of my business philosophy.

One of the core tenets of Enlightened Business is an attitude of equanimity or non-attachment: Do the best you can, but trust that the outcome, whether loss or gain, serves a higher purpose.

When I heard about Icesave going down I tried to practice non-attachment, but the old fear pattern kicked in. To shake off the fear I went on a walk round Regent's Park until I reached a state nearer to equanimity. At least I had placed my savings in a variety of banks in order to spread the risk – I learnt that lesson when I had all of my savings in Northern Rock, the British bank that was nationalised at the beginning of 2008. Intellectual analysis, however, did not help me feel better.

I noticed my breathing and deliberately breathed deeply. I let myself feel the sensations in my body; I was no longer denying the lingering fear but acknowledging its presence and allowing it to flow through my body.

Doing this allowed that energy to dissipate and I began to experience a warm glow. I could then appreciate that I was safe and housed, that I had a loving partner and my belly was full. Taking time to get back in contact with my body and its needs gave me the scope to get a better perspective on the crisis facing me – and the world economy.

Over £4 billion of British savers money had simply 'disappeared'! That's a lot of dosh – but focusing on that didn't help my situation, so I let the thought go. I hoped that the Icelandic Government would do the 'right' thing and return my savings, and for a moment I was angry that they were using my funds to shore up their economy – a true globalised case study if there ever was one. I was also a little cross that the British Government was denying the situation. There were 300,000 British savers in Icesave (one for each Icelander) and yet there was not a word of response from the British government.

What was really getting to me, however, was the perception that I had lost control. Of course I never really had control, but when one has to face this fact directly it's more than uncomfortable – it's a shock to the ego.

Underneath that shock I was fine, but then the self-doubt started to creep in. I had followed my intuition six months ago by depositing funds in Icesave, but I am always aware that what nature has in store and what one thinks is the 'right' outcome might be completely different. So I knew I had to accept and trust whatever was unfolding and to stop trying to *control* things. We *all* did.

Surprisingly (in the circumstances) I slept like a log until about 3am and then my mind started its 'if only' mantra. If *only* I'd got my money out of Icesave earlier; if *only* I'd had less than £50k in my account I would have been covered by the British compensation scheme…maybe I should have gone to the synagogue on Rosh Hashana after all…

I could have listened to my own internal dialogue for the rest of the night, but instead I put my attention on my body and cuddled my partner, then listened to the rhythm of my breath again. I heard my heartbeat. My mind was chattering away somewhere in the distance, but it was getting fainter and fainter and I must have dropped back to slumber because the next thing I knew the sun was beginning to rise behind the bedroom curtains.

The next morning I felt relaxed, happy and calm. Nothing had changed about the outward situation: I'd still lost my money; there was still no word on compensation, but the night had soothed me and everything seemed better than yesterday. There were still uncertainties to deal with, but surely the worst had come…

I was meant to have breakfast with Jonnie, a business friend at George – a posh watering hole for powerful businessmen in Mayfair (I'm not a member – in case you get the wrong idea!). Jonnie was running late when I glanced around and spotted Martin, who runs an advertising conglomerate. We've never been introduced but we know each other by sight, having spent a couple of years staring at each other across the synagogue. I could overhear him talking gloomily to his eating companion: 'Never seen anything like this before, even when…'

Jonnie appeared then, looking distracted and continued Martin's line of thought: 'I don't understand it – where will it end?' He then gave a very simple, yet profound explanation: 'When I grew up, you didn't get debt shoved down your throat – I want to educate my kids to say no to debt…'

That made me think about the credit crunch and how we – that's you and me – all contributed to it. First, we believed that debt was acceptable and that the game was to 'leverage' yourself and your enterprise to the greatest degree in order to complete ever-increasing transactions – and this was mirrored in our personal lives so that we would 'buy' assets way beyond our means should times get hard.

We did this so that we could impress others, rather than feed ourselves, or look after our families and employees. We became shortsighted. It no longer mattered whether the business model was sustainable as long as we could demonstrate quick returns. If the returns didn't materialise quickly enough our backers, or the public markets, would turn against us – and we would be out of a job, or our company would be mopped up by someone with more leverage.

We lost sight of the fun, working all hours and shutting ourselves off from the greater world. We became greedy. Instead of spreading our wealth around either charitably or by creating more jobs in our own organisations (now there's a thought!) we funneled more cash to ourselves and became stressed out in the process. We had become self-centered in our business dealings rather than altruistic, and lost sight of the true *meaning* of business.

To me, having a large bank balance doesn't give as much satisfaction as working in a team, a walk on the beach, or even developing a new product. But we set earning money as the single focus of our working activities and we legally ensured that companies delivered maximum returns (profit equals cash) to shareholders. And then we wondered why the business world had turned out to be such a hostile place.

Although the global markets were still trading, in essence, we were all spiritually bankrupt…

As I left George I checked my Blackberry and there was an email from my friend Victoria. She began: 'Darling…' I was a little shocked as I didn't know her that well, but then I realized she was referring to the British Chancellor of the Exchequer, Alastair Darling. Apparently Darling had now extended the compensation scheme to all Icesave savers, no matter how much money they had in their accounts.

I breathed a sigh of relief. I hadn't lost my savings after all – although I would have to wait a few months – but this was a completely different scenario to the previous day. But what about tomorrow, I wondered? We now live in an uncertain world where the financial market swings wildly in a matter of hours, if not minutes, erasing economies here and creating fresh opportunities there.

Of course, it wasn't meant to be like this. Capitalism was supposed to deliver an increasing standard of living, with wealth cascading down to where it was needed most. And technology was going to create a leisure society with so much free time it would almost be embarrassing. Yet our financial system lurches from crisis to crisis, we work harder than ever and the end goal seems farther and farther away. The rich have gotten wealthier but are they really happy? And the gap between rich and poor is accelerating. In Africa this disparity manifests as crime; in the Middle East as terrorism.

I began this book on an impulse. I felt that the power of business eclipsed governments and that the joy of trading could enhance life and allow the expression and expansion of our destiny. Yet I also felt that something had gone badly wrong with business in general and that unless there was a radical change in the way we treat each other in our transactions, then nature would apply its own 'correction'.

I had no idea that the 'correction' would be happening so soon.

As of Oct 2008 China had $1 trillion dollars invested in U.S. bonds. The U.S. dollar was rising despite the trillions of dollars being printed in order to shore up U.S. banks. Lastly, OPEC members were meeting to discuss cutting back oil production, in order to force oil to a higher price before their economies collapse due to falling prices.

All these events defied received wisdom and yet we still like to believe we were in control of events and there is some science about things. Yet the real science is in nature. Nature has all the answers but we are too arrogant to accept that we cannot act in isolation from it. Intellectually we can understand that we are made of the same atoms as the world around us and are subject to the same forces – yet over the past centuries we have cut ourselves apart from our essential nature.

What we must understand is that the market, like everything else on earth, is an organism. It has its booms, busts and natural cycles. There is an organising power at work, which is greater than any one individual and is quite palpable. It is the same intelligence that produces the various cycles and the complexity of individual cells.

We want to believe that we are totally in control of our lives and everything around us, but to gain maximum effectiveness we need to work with these cycles of nature and the 'spirit' behind them. The market lessons that nature has been trying to teach us since the Great Depression – or one could argue much longer – have clearly not been learnt. We have refused to see the work of nature, or the spiritual side of business – to our own peril.

We won't bring financial stability by doing more of the same thing. Consequently bailing out the banks, lowering interest rates and encouraging lending will only bring temporary relief.

Instead of looking at the global financial meltdown simply in financial terms, we need to step back and see the spiritual emergency currently gripping the markets – and by extension the people. Our business lives and personal aspirations must change. A sustainable world depends on it.

The State of Play

As world leaders and everyday people alike clamour for a global financial system that serves instead of enslaves us, the groundswell for change grows. But what type of new world will it be, and who will make the decision about it? To quote Gordon Brown in the *Washington Post* (Oct 17, 2008) once more:

'This week, European leaders came together to propose the guiding principles that we believe should underpin this new Bretton Woods: transparency, sound banking, responsibility, integrity and global governance. We agreed that urgent decisions implementing these principles should be made to root out the irresponsible and often undisclosed lending at the heart of our problems. To do this, we need cross-border supervision of financial institutions; shared global standards for accounting and regulation; a more responsible approach to executive remuneration that rewards hard work, effort and enterprise but not irresponsible risk-taking; and the renewal of our international institutions to make them effective early-warning systems for the world economy.'

Brave and inspiring words, but just a few months later Governments were doing anything possible – including printing money – to encourage a return to the *old* system.

Earlier I asked you to consider company consciousness and to evaluate what role you and your company play in the evolutionary process. Now I ask you to consider your part in manifesting the New Global Age and how you can become involved in enterprises that are both profitable and life-enhancing.

We've discussed that money on its own does not lead to ongoing fulfilment. We know from experience that we feel good when we are doing good. It's not rocket science. If we help a stranger cross the road, or do someone a favour (without an agenda), then we have an inner glow. If they flash us a warm smile so much the better, but if they offered us a tip (the capitalist principle again) we might feel insulted.

So the first change we need to make to our existing system is to realise we are part of an ecosystem in which everyone is connected. If the polarity between rich and poor continues, the world will become more unstable. We are already experiencing what happens when fundamentalist organisations step in to provide basic services and infrastructure in developing countries: they rapidly recruit new members.

The second change is to ensure that we do not add to the world's troubles by siphoning off natural resources from a community simply to make executives and shareholders rich. We also cannot continue to cause environmental and cultural damage without regard for the consequences. This may seem quixotic in today's hard-nosed business environment, but if we want our grandchildren and their heirs to enjoy the lifestyle we have taken for granted (or something similar but more sustainable) we have to wake up to our responsibilities.

So what can we do in our businesses to bring ourselves in line with nature as an antidote to these increasingly greater and more worrying economic cycles? Well for a start we can stop looking enviously at our peers and instead look compassionately at our workers.

Spread It Around

Have you noticed how everyone seems stressed and overworked? Have you considered what it would be like if there were more people doing the same work? Hold that thought while I tell you a (true) story.

On Indian train stations there is always a chai stall and the chai is served in clay cups. Once the chai is drunk, the ritual is to smash the cup onto the floor where it fractures into a thousand pieces. Then the station sweeper comes along, collects the pieces and they get recycled. This ritual is aesthetic (the cups look and feel good and the chai tastes better); environmentally pleasing (100% recycling) and it creates work for the sweepers and the cup manufacturers.

Then some bright spark decided to modernise and abolish the tradition and replace the clay with plastic. The result: jobs were threatened and the stations became littered with unsightly cups. Commuters were just chucking the cups anywhere and of course they do not biodegrade for centuries. Eventually, along came a new Minister for Railways who legislated against the use of plastic (can you imagine that?!) and brought back the clay cups.

Now when I tell Western business people this story, most of them start calculating the incremental cost of employing more people in the production process. Surely this is inefficient and uneconomic, they say. But hang on! One of the most incredible gifts one can give someone is the opportunity to earn a living!

So let's pick up our thread again. Why not offer the most harassed of your staff additional human resources AND insist they work a sensible day AND give someone the opportunity to work? And why not pay for it out of your pay!

Do yourself a favour and calculate the difference between your pay last year and that of your average employee. Yes, I bet you were expecting me to calculate your pay relative to your lowest paid employee – but I think it is enough just to compare yourself to the average wage. I'm not going to tell you what the 'right' ratio is. Just do the calculation and see how you feel. If you're embarrassed by the answer, then you're paying yourself too much!

And yes, this is a novel approach and you'll be a trailblazer. The pay-off? You'll be a corporate hero. You'll feel good about yourself, your kids and partner will be proud of you and instead of your friends hearing about your remuneration with envy, they'll want to emulate you in a way that they can rather than competitively.

And you might even be asked to the Inauguration of the next US President... Leonard Abess, a Florida bank president, was invited to attend the Inauguration of President Obama because he took his $60 million bonus and gave it out to all 399 employees and 72 former employees!

Do Something For Someone Else

The backdrop to the credit crunch is self-centredness. When you are seeking nothing but fulfillment for others through your vocation, then naturally your attention will flow outwards and you'll start noticing how you can be of service. This produces a real and tangible connection to the universe.

I actually was aware that during my own little credit drama, I had become more inward. I also felt the fear of loss. In order to counteract that, I sought out beggars, even the most disreputable ones and thrust money into their cups. In one or two instances the recipients were too doped to notice. Which is another interesting discussion point, because there is a great debate about whether to give to beggars or not. In fact, my local authority has an advertising campaign goading people not to give anything ever, because, they say, the money will be turned into drugs and more harm will be done.

I take an opposing view. I don't believe it is for me to judge others. Yes, the money could be used for drugs, but shunning a human being is hardly going to inspire them to start a new life. I prefer to think that this small interaction and show of compassion can be the turning point.

Spiritual teachers always stress inclusiveness and some go out of their way to find disadvantaged people and interact with them. Why don't you try it yourself?

Keep it Local

It is often argued that multinationals like Starbucks, McDonalds, and Walmart not only destroy local economies, they produce cultural monotony and suck money out of nation-states into the hands of private shareholders wherever they are based. This may be true, but it doesn't have to be like this. The most effective solution is not, however, in attempting to pass unenforceable laws, electing media politicans, or by rioting or boycotts. In the capitalist system the most effective response we have is our individual buying power.

In *Tescopoly* by Andrew Simms, the philosopher Alain de Botton writes about the international supermarket chain Tesco:

'What should be done about Tesco? Many critics want the place banned and hemmed in by regulation... But ultimately the real trick is not to ban such places, but to create different desires in consumers, to reach a situation where people are sufficiently sensitive to the drawbacks of Tesco or McDonald's that they don't want to shop there.'

But there is more to it than that, and in addition we must take into account the benefits of multi-nationals. Trading between nations also increases understanding and tolerance. Multinationals COULD channel their profits back into local communities, and they could buy from local suppliers –it's just that because they are chasing the short-term lowest cost profit objective, instead of the holistic long-term vision, they DON'T – well, not normally.

While it is easy to assert that consumers can simply stop supporting companies that do 'bad' things, what consumers choose may not ultimately be 'best'. So we see also the rise of junk food and consumption of cigarettes, which clearly are detrimental to long-term health, but are still very popular.

International trade is fantastic when there is a real interchange between different cultures – each providing the other with goods and services that enhance life. Exporting one culture globally, destroying indigenous cultures, ruining natural habitats and creating a boring uni-dimensional world will not be tolerated and is not being tolerated by the cosmos. Transporting produce, lathered in preservatives and schlepping it across the planet is plain or should I say, plane dumb.

Setting up a call centre in India to service clients in Cleveland does nothing for anyone. It takes jobs away from local companies and ironically overpays the Indians, who then take on Western standards of drink, drug abuse and inhuman hours.

This is not to discourage international trading, far from it. It's just that the communities trading should both be winners. When jobs in one country are decimated through outsourcing, there can only be toxic damaging effects for all involved.

I was very encouraged by an interview I heard recently on BBC World Service with Andrew Whitty, new CEO of GSK. Firstly GSK is making a small number of its drugs (including an anti-malarial 'medicine'), available at a 45% discount to people in the fifty poorest countries. Second, GSK has put information about 800 drugs into a patent pool to be shared with others. Thirdly GSK is ploughing back 25% of its profits in the least developed countries into building health-care infrastructure.

Whitty was straightforward in his acknowledgement that this was a small step and that he hoped other large drug companies would follow his example. But personally, I think this is a huge initiative because it demonstrates a connection – at last – between a large multinational, its market and a responsibility to act as a 'global citizen', to use Whitty's own words.

It also shows that multi-nationals are not necessarily 'bad'. As I have argued previously, all it takes is a change at the top to bring around a change of consciousness in the whole company.

It's time to become idealistic again. We can all make a difference. Every job we create feeds a family. Every pure product or service we sell enhances life and makes us feel better about ourselves.

We seem to have lost the basic connection with the true meaning of life. One of the most notable features of my savings 'crisis' is that the world carried on just as before, and when I stopped giving attention to the whinging voice in my head and began to pay attention to what was happening outside, my satisfaction and wonder increased dramatically.

There is nothing wrong with personal ambition, indeed it can be a driver to great achievement, but when that is all there is, it leads to a one dimensional world. Let's use the current global credit crisis as an opportunity to make our world a more integrated, fulfilled and colourful place.

If you're not passionate about your career, use this moment to set a new course, one that fulfills you 100 percent.

Balanced Profits and Growth

Tim Jackson of the Sustainable Development Commission, writes in his report *Prosperity Without Growth?* :

'Our reliance on debt to finance the cycle of growth has created a deeply unstable system which has made individuals, families and communities inherently vulnerable to cycles of boom and bust, while increasing consumption does not make us happier.'

The most fundamental change required is to expand company objectives so that profit (which must remain a key objective) must be derived from responsible principles:

- Your company must have holistic values.
- Your remuneration should be balanced by the necessity to ensure profit objectives that do not compromise more holistic values.
- Products should be life-supporting and not manufactured in a way that is harmful to the environment.
- Profits should be distributed amongst shareholders and the communities that produce them – just as companies like GSK are beginning to do.

The vast financial packages currently commanded by captains of industry – particularly in America, even when their companies are in trouble – are at odds with the principles of Enlightened Business and modesty. Out of proportion remuneration leads to fear (of its loss), inflation of ego and attention on self rather than others. Accumulation of too much wealth leads to toxicity. Healthy and wealthy individuals become philanthropic by nature as their souls realise that holding on to wealth (rather than using it to create opportunities for others) carries an inherent spiritual danger.

Again to avoid misunderstanding, there is nothing 'wrong' with having and making billions, or striving to do so. However riches require a strong and integrated personality, otherwise they work against the psyche, causing unhappiness and a feeling of pointlessness.

Public Market Caution

Although we may be egalitarian, we have to recognise that in the era of transformation in which we are currently living we are very fortunate to have the time and opportunity to consider the 'bigger' issues and to set an example to others in how we live our business lives.

Public markets encourage institutions (at best) and individuals (at worst) to invest in businesses in which they (mostly) have little understanding. Investors and shareholders require you to maximise profits – that is the Number One Rule of Traditional Capitalism.

It is true that the larger institutions will research investment opportunities with care, but even these are now increasingly at the mercy of those seeking short-term gain, who have little interest in the long-term viability of individual companies. Individual investors too, seek to 'invest' their savings and improve on the more 'pedestrian' returns available via bank savings.

Therefore, if you want to be true to spiritual business, you cannot have the 'traditional' shareholder base. It won't work – as was proved by Anita Roddick and The Body Shop, whose campaigning led to continuous tensions with the public marketplace where its shares were traded. Raising money in the public marketplace is not appropriate unless the objectives of the company are clearly articulated during the fundraising.

However it is my observation that a growing number of investors are interested in ensuring their money is used for life-enhancing ends – but as with any time of transition, this is balanced by a growing number of speculators whose only objective is to make a quick buck.

Currency speculators brought down governments at the end of the 20th century and now hedge funds place heavy bets on share prices, which then fluctuate wildly in the face of rumour and look like bringing down the global financial system in the 21st century.

Empowerment and Company Education

The Adam Smith philosophy of 'Division of Labour' certainly enhanced productivity during the Industrial Revolution, but repetitive tasks should be left to machines, not people. And although technology and service industries have replaced manufacturing to a great extent in the developed world, 'Adam Smith thinking' still prevails. Human thinking in general continues to define the physical world in Newtonian terms, simultaneously physicists are saying that the quantum world around us is interconnected.

Satisfaction in life comes from being involved in an entire process, not simply a part of it, but our whole education system is towards specialisation at the cost of generalisation. In companies this culture has led to a business being broken down into separate departments: Head Office, Customer Sales, Customer Service, Marketing, Training, Human Resources, Technology, Public Affairs, Accounts, etc.

It is obvious that each of us has strong and weak points, but this specialisation does nothing to enhance an overall consciousness of the business. Instead it often leads to warring fiefdoms, especially in large corporations. As I've mentioned, I spent much of my time after my company was acquired working my way through the labyrinth of corporate politics at the expense of my creativity and productiveness. Isn't it time to have a second look at the effectiveness of assembly-line specialisation?

For a company to reach maximum creative expression there has to be a real attempt to utilise the many different talents each employee brings to the organisation, as well as ensuring everyone imbibes the company ethos and is encouraged to feedback their concerns and delights. And this philosophy must be transferred to everywhere the enterprise operates.

It is simple to set up a sweatshop overseas, and easy to justify its existence by believing it's providing income to poor villagers. But the exploitation of foreign workers and the expectation that they will continue to do dehumanizing work is not acceptable. A villager in India is just as entitled to dignity and fulfilling work as if he were in a neighbouring town to the company HQ.

Technological Utopia?

We can see that a new global paradigm has been manifesting for a long time and there has been a generational shift from the physical world of agriculture to the Industrial Revolution and then the 'softer' wireless world of the mobile phone and internet. Around 150 years ago there were no TV channels, broadband or even radio. Now cyberspace is filling at an ever-increasing rate and this trend is inevitable because it mirrors the rise of global consciousness itself.

This is a natural phenomenon – rather than lead by a conscious endeavour by humans – as much as we would like to believe this myth.

We take it as commonplace that we can speak, email or text anyone at anytime anywhere. We can send money instantaneously, thus facilitating electronic trading. We can establish friendships with people we will never meet face to face, or go on a virtual holiday. Mobile phones can be utilised to circulate breaking news round the globe or to record a song for YouTube. We can shop for music online and a computer will suggest other recordings for our enjoyment. We can participate in a social networking chat-room, bid for concert tickets, receive directions from Google, and see satellite images of our proposed holiday destination or trade shares. All from the comfort of our homes.

Computers bridge the gap between consciousness and the physical world because they allow us to act remotely simply using thought. Past generations would never have understood this action at a distance. The online virtual space Second Life, for example, defies all the norms of the 'conventional' living patterns of the past. Nobody (outside of the science fiction fraternity) could have predicted how many hours would be spent as an avatar or how virtual land would be bought and sold.

Technology is another manifestation of our consciousness and part of the natural rhythm of the universe. It is through technology that business has rapidly transformed separate nation-states into an interdependent world economy and there is every indication that this drive towards unity will only complexify in the future.

Self-Referral and Unity

The first trend I predict is a growing realisation that we really are connected to each other and to the planet in a much more profound way than we have previously been aware.

Already we have seen how multi-national companies have grown, and how financial markets are globally connected so that market conditions in America follow through to volatility in Asia, with computers able to conduct trade automatically. The chaos that ensues is a direct consequence of the lack of self-referral so common in our society.

Technology has made us conscious on a global level. The elections in

Zimbabwe and the Olympics in China have both been influenced by our ability to watch events live and as they unfold. No longer can atrocities be hidden – at least not for too long. In addition to conventional news channels, which are increasingly hosting blogs and other forms of participatory journalism and feedback, websites like Avaaz.org can provide a different insight and the ability to influence global events and world trade.

It is wonderful that trading is taking place between nations, but so often there is a winner and a loser. Outsourcing, for example, was big news. What better way to enhance profit than by outsourcing a call-centre to India? Fire local call centre staff, overpay people in a developing country, corrupt them with western values, temporarily raise their income and when they become too expensive move on to a cheaper territory, dumping them in the process – and all courtesy of new technology!

We could look at the current uncertain times as a threat to our stability. Alternatively, we could regard them as nature's wake-up call to shock us to no longer worry about what others feel about us and instead get satisfaction from within. We can also begin to understand the role nature has in store for us and become enthusiastic to play our part.

True Liberation

Technology was supposed to set us free, but instead it has enslaved us. No longer is there a working week and a sacrosanct time for sleep and family. It is considered legitimate and even admirable to work long hours and be contactable 24/7 even on holiday. It has become socially acceptable to bring work home, but rarely to bring kids to the office – especially if you're a man.

How can we use technology to liberate ourselves in business? Simply by using it to be ourselves, rather than to hide. In the coming years, consumers and employees will appreciate truthfulness, transparency and simplicity more than ever. Enlightened Business will enhance our consciousness so that work becomes part of our lives, rather than our lives being part of work.

To quote John Naish, author of *Enough: Breaking Free from the World of More*, in the *London Times* of 23 October 2008: 'The new cool will involve personal sustainability – investing carefully in hardy, well-made items that are made to last and used faithfully for donkey's years – not evanescent stuff from Primark grabbed and chucked in a series of one-night shopping stands.'

In short, the age of technology for mass-production and mass-marketing is over, because it does not represent authentic trading. Authentic trading must involve every aspect of manufacturing being fulfilling. Thus there will be liberation from production lines, call-centres and blandness and a return to basic trading values – whilst the internet will be harnessed to sell well-made products to mass-markets.

Clean Technology

The level of discovery we are currently witnessing directly mirrors the level of our own consciousness. If we are not connected to the consequences of our actions, then our discoveries can produce toxic side-effects.

Many modern inventions I am aware of are produced in isolation of their overall effects: The combustion engine pollutes; the waste from nuclear energy cannot be disposed of easily; chemotherapy kills good cells as well as cancerous. Electricity is the lifeblood of modern living, but we rely too heavily on depleting fossil fuels to produce it.

The fact is that technology is not being harnessed in a conscious way to uplift us. The ramifications are ever increasing crises in the environment and climate, and the madness of nuclear warfare – where a nation feels safe because it has a weapon that can completely destroy another nation (several times over!) and spread contamination over the entire planet.

We are recognising these shortcomings in our current technology and in the future we will see business focus on technologies that are 'clean'.

A report from Morgan Stanley, published in the fall of 2007 stated:

'The global risks posed by climate change are driving spending and investment in clean energy solutions, which (unlike the oil shock that spawned the first wave of alternative energy solutions in the 1970s) is durable and accelerating. In our upside scenario, we believe the annual clean energy revenue opportunity could reach $500 billion in 2020 and $1 trillion in 2030.

We believe the pipeline of innovations will provide new clean energy solutions for many years to come. We believe we have just entered the second of four waves of clean energy innovation that will span the first two or three decades of the 21st century.'

This is a tremendous market opportunity for every level of entrepreneurial activity and which will have global significance.

Nature is telling us we need to lessen our dependence on depleting fossil fuels oil and to take responsibility for the pollution we are unleashing on the planet and it is 'talking' to us in many languages; market forces and climate change being two of its dialects.

Unfortunately, the environment has become a political issue in recent times, but the situation is too urgent not to act. Climate change is all around us and nobody fully understands the causes, but this does not change the situation. Anyone with an enlightened perspective can see that producing energy from expensive, polluting, limited resources is just plain dumb.

You can choose whatever reason you like for becoming involved in clean sustainable energy projects. It could be making money, or concern that the destruction of the rain forests will eventually make our planet uninhabitable. It could be the challenge of finding a clean solution to the world's energy needs – it is not just about being environmentally responsible. Nature is motivating us to become creative and take our thinking to a new connected level – and the stakes are being raised every second.

So Where Do We Look For Solutions?

The first place to look for solutions to our current global crisis is nature itself. Before man came along nature was very efficient at self-regulation. For example, the monsoons in India were so regular that the date of the beginning of the monsoon in each city could be printed in a diary! Occasionally a monsoon would 'fail'. This would be every 15 years or so – but the next year the monsoon would return 'on schedule'. That was until about five years ago, when the start of the monsoon and its length became unpredictable for the first time in living memory.

We tend to focus on the (considerable) downside of this, without recognising the tremendous intelligence in nature's software that is responsible for organising the cycles that we see all around us. So instead of fighting nature, why not try harnessing this intelligence and building it into our systems?

This is exactly the stance taken by the 'new' science of bio-mimicry, which is the 'science of developing sustainable technologies inspired by ideas from nature' (see www.biomimicryinstitute.org). Here is a quote from the biomimicry website:

'Like the viceroy butterfly imitating the monarch, we humans are imitating the best adapted organisms in our habitat. We are learning, for instance, how to harness energy like a leaf, grow food like a prairie, build ceramics like an abalone, self-medicate like a chimp, create color like a peacock, compute like a cell, and run a business like a hickory forest.'

In other words, biomimicry accepts that the world has been evolving for four billion years and starts from an assumption that nature might have something to teach us! It is extraordinary to me that we are arrogant enough as species to believe that we have to start all inventions with a blank piece of paper from first principles, without observing that nature has infinite intelligence and is able to produce extraordinary progress without harmful side effects – with the exception of the human race.

Because humans have the free will to override nature they are also able to produce an enormous amount of damage to themselves and the environment. But I have no doubt that man is dispensable and that the crises that we experience in the environment, financial markets and culturally will become so great that we risk destroying ourselves unless we wake up and seize the amazing opportunities that we are currently confronted by.

User-Generated Trading

The global marketplace offers unparalleled opportunities for those who understand that the need for self-sufficiency, coupled with new technology, will accelerate a move towards User Generated Trade.

This is not to say that large companies will disappear, but that increasingly they will struggle to compete against passionate, smaller organisations who will use the internet to go direct to market. For example, my partner just bought a pair of warm sheepskin boots via the internet from the NZ Nature Company.

At present we have a schizoid attitude towards this form of trade. On the one hand we want to encourage 'traditional' trading where we buy direct from the producer. Be it coffee from Brazil, furniture from Thailand or boots from New Zealand. But of course, we worry about all that fuel. I am confident that several of the current clean fuel initiatives will deliver fruit and also that in the meantime, aware retailers will use energy-efficient means of transportation.

Where will this leave the large multi-nationals? At the moment companies are becoming bigger and bigger. Banks around the world are merging at a frenetic rate and this trend will be followed in all sectors as financial security will be the primary concern amongst those left with a job.

However tension in those companies that refuse to evolve will increase as executives become ever further removed from their customers. I'm still old enough to remember when I had a personal bank manager whom I would meet on a regular basis. For those with cash to burn, you will now have a wealth manager. But the less well-heeled will have to make do with a call centre. Paradoxically, the really poor but entrepreneurial in Africa and Bangladesh will have a personally managed micro-loan (and stand a 97% chance or higher of paying it back).

As consumers recognise the absurdity of buying a product because of its packaging or because it is endorsed by a 'celebrity'; as creative people understand that they need to be themselves and in control of their own destinies and as e-tailing overtakes mall-shopping in popularity, then we will see a radical change in the business world. Because the same technology which allows electronic money to be flashed round the world in a instant is transforming the very nature of business.

I am not alone in spotting this radical change. The current online advertising market is estimated by Kelsey Group to have reached $45 billion and is forecast to reach $147 billion by 2012. And the Internet Measurement Retail Group (IMRG) predicts that in the United Kingdom by 2018, online retailing will represent half of all retail sales.

A Call to Action

So as an enlightened businessperson how can you have a fulfilling career in the new global marketplace?

Stop worrying about certainty! Life was never certain. You've always wanted more excitement but you found it on TV by immersing yourself in the lives of others, or by comparing yourself enviously to your peers. Now you can have a 'real' life. Living a full life does not mean 'having', it means 'being'. It means being connected to nature, to your family and friends. It means trading with people you know, whether they live up the road or around the globe.

Sure there will still be plenty of people out there prepared to slog away for nameless shareholders, but that doesn't need to be you. The universe is providing countless opportunities for you to express yourself. And you don't have to do it alone either.

I have mentioned the demise of multi-nationals, but those that practise honesty and that empower individual business units will survive, and you can still choose a place for yourself within an enlightened company.

You could worry about the future or you could use this time to transform yourself into who you really are.

We look around us at the growing climate variance, increasing natural disasters and unpredictability of the markets and we wonder aloud what we can do. Then we look outside ourselves. We expect government to save us; we blame other people; we blame multi-nationals, arms manufacturers, supermarkets and drug companies as if they were separate.

But they are us.

Over to Us!

At the World Trade Organisation's Ministerial meeting in Seattle in 1999, 40,000 or more people protested against globalisation. Likewise, the Rainforest Action Network (RAN) embarrasses corporations to become more accountable.

For example, RAN claims to have spurred Citigroup into setting up a lending policy that takes into account the environment. And in 2006, RAN helped stop the Texas utility company TXU from developing 11 new coal-fired power plants by going directly to the project's financiers, dressing as 'Billionaires for Coal' and protesting outside bank branches across the country.

But activist initiatives like these, although admirable in their outcomes, do not address the central cause of these policies – which is the lack of consciousness and connection with the outcome of executive initiatives. These initiatives fail to factor in the harm that is being done to the executives themselves in their emotional lives and to the environments that they are destroying.

The simple fact is that we are living on borrowed time and although we may be able to live a comfortable life, it is debatable if our grandchildren will have such a privilege unless we as executives take an honest look at our activities.

Perhaps the CEO of the company paying poor wages, with appalling labour relations went to your school and now lives a few miles away. His Chairman may be a member of your gym. The Board members take vacation near where you hang out in the summer. And the executives who report to the Board play tennis with your chums...

The Board itself reports to shareholders. But who are they? They're people just like you – or maybe they're pension funds. But whose pension are they managing? Your friends' pensions. And where do these shareholders eat? Probably not at McDonalds. Most likely they find a good neighbourhood restaurant serving organic food – I suspect they may shop at Whole Foods.

But hang on, who am I describing? Why, it could be YOU!

This is the mystery of our current dilemma. The resolution of our world crisis is in our hands but as long as we externalise the problem and blame 'them', we are trapped in a prison of our own consciousness – and how crazy is that? Most executives don't want inner conflict, they want to be themselves and to uphold values they can be proud of. But in corporations, particularly large ones, something takes over. It may be the fear of being different when they are actually the same as everyone else.

We are far more powerful than we think we are, but in our dithering and fear we have forgotten our power.

Now it's time to remember your destiny, to embrace Enlightened Business and help transform the world!

What will you chose?

I wish you well on your journey and hope that your business life is filled with fulfillment and satisfaction for you and those around you. I hope your career is also exciting and fun and that you achieve extraordinary rewards both financially and spiritually!

WORKBOOK:

The first change we need to make to our existing system is a sense of genuine compassion and a realisation that we are here to help humanity as a whole via our business endeavours. We are part of an ecosystem in which everyone is connected. List some ways that you connect to people within your organisation, and how it then connects to the world around it. How do these relationships make you FEEL?

_____

_____

_____

_____

_____

_____

_____

_____

Do not add to the world's troubles by siphoning off natural resources from a community simply to make executives and shareholders rich. We also cannot continue to cause environmental and cultural damage without regard for the consequences. List some ways in which your company has minimised its impact on the environment, or adapted to the current credit crisis. If it hasn't done either write out a list of how it might adapt to these challenges!

_____

_____

_____

_____

_____

_____

_____

_____

List some examples of a time when you did something For Someone Else. When you are seeking nothing but fulfillment for others through your vocation, then naturally your attention will flow outwards and you'll start noticing how you can be of service. This produces a real and tangible connection to the universe.

_____

_____

_____

_____

_____

_____

Keep it Local. Examine how your company shows respect to those communities that produce your profits and how you could plough some of that wealth back to its originators.

_____
_____
_____
_____
_____
_____
_____
_____

Become idealistic again. We can all make a difference. Every job we create feeds a family. Every pure product or service we sell enhances life and makes us feel better about ourselves. Take the time here to list the ways in which YOU can become enlivened in the business cycle to be the best you can be. Use this list as your own personal mission statement for Enlightened Business, and see where it takes you!

_____
_____
_____
_____
_____
_____
_____
_____
_____

Acknowledgements

Thank you Daniel and Simon. Watching your first steps in business encourages me to think Enlightened Business is making a comeback!

Thank you Luiza for your love, support and positivity.

Thank you Lesley for supporting me through my most difficult challenges.

Thanks Etienne for your kind quote and for being a fellow traveller.

Thanks Cathal for the publicity and Jeremy for your way with words and for being a friend and sounding board.

Thanks to Rak for helping me turn vague ideas into solid concepts.

And thanks to all those I have the good fortune to meet in business. You have taught me so much and without you this book could not have been written.

Index

Lightning Source UK Ltd.
Milton Keynes UK
17 January 2011

165834UK00004B/67/P